GENERAL VIEW OF THE AGRICULTURE OF HERTFORDSHIRE

GENERAL VIEW of the AGRICULTURE of HERTFORDSHIRE

A Reprint of the Work Drawn up for the
Consideration of the Board of Agriculture
and Internal Improvement

by

ARTHUR YOUNG

Secretary of the Board

DAVID & CHARLES REPRINTS

ISBN 0 7153 4778 0

This book was first published in 1804
This edition published in 1971

Printed in Great Britain by
Clarke Doble & Brendon Limited Plymouth
for David & Charles (Publishers) Limited
South Devon House Railway Station
Newton Abbot Devon

GENERAL VIEW

OF THE

AGRICULTURE

OF

HERTFORDSHIRE.

GENERAL VIEW

OF THE

AGRICULTURE

OF

HERTFORDSHIRE.

DRAWN UP FOR THE CONSIDERATION OF

THE BOARD OF AGRICULTURE

AND INTERNAL IMPROVEMENT.

———◆———

BY

THE SECRETARY OF THE BOARD.

═══════════

LONDON:

PRINTED BY B. McMILLAN, BOW-STREET, COVENT-GARDEN,
PRINTER TO HIS ROYAL HIGHNESS THE PRINCE OF WALES;
FOR G. AND W. NICOL, PALL-MALL, BOOKSELLERS TO HIS
MAJESTY, AND THE BOARD OF AGRICULTURE; AND SOLD
BY G. AND J. ROBINSON, PATERNOSTER-ROW;
J. ASPERNE, CORNHILL; CADELL AND DAVIES,
STRAND; W. CREECH, EDINBURGH; AND
JOHN ARCHER, DUBLIN.

1804.

ADVERTISEMENT.

THE great desire that has been very generally expressed, for having the AGRICULTURAL SURVEYS of the KINGDOM reprinted, with the additional Communications which have been received since the ORIGINAL REPORTS were circulated, has induced the BOARD OF AGRICULTURE to come to a resolution of reprinting such as may appear on the whole fit for publication. It is proper at the same time to add, that the Board does not consider itself responsible for any fact or observation contained in the Reports thus reprinted, as it is impossible to consider them yet in a perfect state ; and that it will thankfully acknowledge any additional information which may still be communicated : an invitation, of which, it is hoped, many will avail themselves, as there is no circumstance from which any one can derive more real satisfaction, than that of contributing, by every possible means, to promote the improvement of his Country.

N. B. *Letters to the Board, may be addressed to Lord* SHEFFIELD, *the President, No.* 32, *Sackville-Street, Piccadilly, London.*

PLAN

FOR RE-PRINTING THE

AGRICULTURAL SURVEYS.

BY THE PRESIDENT OF THE BOARD OF AGRICUL-
TURE.

=====

A BOARD established for the purpose of making every essential inquiry into the Agricultural State, and the means of promoting the internal improvement of a powerful Empire, will necessarily have it in view to examine the sources of public prosperity, in regard to various important particulars. Perhaps the following is the most natural order for carrying on such important investigations; namely, to ascertain,

1. The riches to be obtained from the surface of the national territory.

2. The mineral or subterraneous treasures of which the country is possessed.

3. The wealth to be derived from its streams, rivers, canals, inland navigations, coasts, and fisheries ;— and

4. The means of promoting the improvement of the people, in regard to their health, industry, and morals, founded on a *statistical* survey, or a minute and careful inquiry into the actual state of every parochial district in the kingdom, and the circumstances of its inhabitants.

Under

Under one or other of these heads, every point of real importance that can tend to promote the general happiness of a great nation, seems to be included.

Investigations of so extensive and so complicated a nature, must require, it is evident, a considerable space of time before they can be completed. Differing indeed in many respects from each other, it is better perhaps that they should be undertaken at different periods, and separately considered. Under that impression, the Board of Agriculture has hitherto directed its attention to the first point only, namely, the cultivation of the surface, and the resources to be derived from it.

That the facts essential for such an investigation might be collected with more celerity and advantage, a number of intelligent and respectable individuals were appointed, to furnish the Board with accounts of the state of husbandry, and the means of improving the different districts of the kingdom. The returns they sent were printed, and circulated by every means the Board of Agriculture could devise, in the districts to which they respectively related; and in consequence of that circulation, a great mass of additional valuable information has been obtained. For the purpose of communicating that information to the Public in general, but more especially to those Counties the most interested therein, the Board has resolved to re-print the Survey of each County, as soon as it seemed to be fit for publication; and, among several equally advanced, the Counties of Norfolk and Lancaster were pitched upon for the commencement of the proposed publication; it being thought most advisable to begin with one County on the Eastern, and another on the Western Coast of the island. When all these Surveys shall have been thus re-printed, it will be attended with little difficulty to draw up

an

an abstract of the whole (which will not probably exceed two or three volumes quarto) to be laid before HIS MAJESTY, and both Houses of Parliament; and afterwards, a General Report on the present state of the country, and the means of its improvement, may be systematically arranged, according to the various subjects connected with Agriculture. Thus every individual in the kingdom may have,

1. An account of the husbandry of his own particular county ; or,

2. A general view of the agricultural state of the kingdom at large, according to the counties, or districts, into which it is divided; or,

3. An arranged system of information on agricultural subjects, whether accumulated by the Board since its establishment, or previously known:

And thus information respecting the state of the kingdom, and agricultural knowledge in general, will be attainable with every possible advantage.

In re-printing these Reports, it was judged necessary, that they should be drawn up according to one uniform model; and after fully considering the subject, the following form was pitched upon, as one that would include in it all the particulars which it was necessary to notice in an Agricultural Survey. As the other Reports will be re-printed in the same manner, the reader will thus be enabled to find out at once where any point is treated of, to which he may wish to direct his attention.

PLAN OF THE RE-PRINTED REPORTS.

---

* Where the quantity is considerable, the information respecting the crops commonly cultivated may be arranged under the following heads—for example, Wheat :

1. Preparation { tillage, manure. }
2. Sort.
3. Steeping.
4. Seed (quantity sown).
5. Time of sowing.

6. Culture whilst growing { hoe, weeding, feeding. }
7. Harvest.
8. Threshing.
9. Produce.
10. Manufacture of bread.

In general, the same heads will suit the following grains :

Barley. Oats. Beans. Rye. Pease. Buck-wheat.

Vetches — Application.

Cole-seed — { Feeding, Seed. }

Turnips — { Drawn, Fed, Fed on grass, —— in houses. }

Chap.

CHAP.

PERFECTION in such inquiries is not in the power of any body of men to obtain at once, whatever may be the extent of their views or the vigour of their exertions. If LOUIS XIV. eager to have his kingdom known, and possessed of boundless power to effect it, failed so much in the attempt, that of all the provinces in his kingdom, only one was so described as to secure the approbation of posterity*, it will not be thought strange that a Board, possessed

---

* See VOLTAIRE's Age of LOUIS XIV. vol. ii. p. 127, 128, edit. 1752. The following extract from that work will explain the circumstance above alluded to :

" LOUIS had no COLBERT, nor LOUVOIS, when, about the year 1698, for the instruction of the Duke of BURGUNDY, he ordered each of the intendants to draw up a particular description of his province. By this means an exact account of the kingdom might have been obtained, and a just enumeration of the inhabitants. It was an useful work, though all the intendants had not the capacity and attention of Monsieur DE LAMOIGNON DE BAVILLE. Had what the King directed been as well executed, in regard to
every

sessed of means so extremely limited, should find it difficult
to reach even that degree of perfection which perhaps
might have been attainable with more extensive powers.
The candid reader cannot expect in these Reports more
than a certain portion of useful information, so arranged as
to render them a basis for further and more detailed inquiries. The attention of the intelligent cultivators of the
kingdom, however, will doubtless be excited, and the minds
of men in general gradually brought to consider favoura-
bly of an undertaking which will enable all to contribute
to the national stores of knowledge, upon topics so truly
interesting as those which concern the agricultural interests of their country ; interests which, on just principles,
never can be improved, until the present state of the kingdom is fully known, and the means of its future improvement ascertained with minuteness and accuracy.

every province, as it was by this magistrate in the account of Languedoc, the
collection would have been one of the most valuable monuments of the age.
Some of them are well done ; but the plan was irregular and imperfect, because
all the intendants were not restrained to one and the same. It were to be
wished that each of them had given, in columns, the number of inhabitants
n each election; the nobles, the citizens, the labourers, the artisans, the
mechanics; the cattle of every kind ; the good, the indifferent, and the bad
lands ; all the clergy, regular and secular; their revenues, those of the towns,
and those of the communities.

" All these heads, in most of their accounts, are confused and imperfect ;
and it is frequently necessary to search with great care and pains, to find what
is wanted. The design was excellent, and would have been of the greatest use,
had it been executed with judgment and uniformity."

PREFACE.

THE County of Hertford had made considerable improvements in Agriculture at the commencement of the last century. Ellis, of Little Gaddesden, published his numerous works about sixty or seventy years since : they were abridged in 1772; in which abridgement, the Editor justly observes, " that the spirited prac-
" tices of excellent common husbandry which of
" late years have made much noise, are clearly
" ascertained by him, their merit stated, and
" their conduct explained. The best turnip and
" clover husbandry are particularly set forth, as
" practically as they can be at this day; the
" whole conduct of manures with practical pre-
" cision. A full knowledge of the use of soiling
" horses and cattle with tares, clover, &c. ;
" saving the drainings of the farm-yard, form-
" ing composts, the variations of soils, which
" require corresponding variations of manure and
" tillage (an article of great importance, and
" fully treated by no other writer), and the
" whole management of sheep, are among many
" other instances." These practices he drew almost entirely from the common management of Hertfordshire, at a period when several of
them

them were wholly unknown in other districts. Such were the improvements of this County, by which its Agriculture arrived to a certain degree of perfection, then superior to the rest of England. Since that time, other Counties, and Norfolk in particular, have followed this example; while Hertfordshire has effected little more than the rest, if we except the cultivation of Swedish turnips, in which this County has uncommon merit ; for I cannot but consider her other exertions as little more than the result of national prosperity, equally extended in agricultural improvements over the whole kingdom.

In regard to the information which I have been able to procure, I flatter myself that the following pages will not be found barren. Had the experiments of individuals been more extensive, this Report might have been more complete. I have endeavoured to render it as perfect and comprehensive as those experiments would permit.

The Reader will observe, that different extracts are inserted in this Work from Mr. WALKER's printed Report of this County ; such passages are marked with inverted commas.

CONTENTS.

CONTENTS.

CHAPTER I.   GEOGRAPHICAL STATE.

CONTENTS.

AGRICULTURAL SURVEY

OF

HERTFORDSHIRE.

CHAPTER I.

GEOGRAPHICAL STATE.

SECTION I.—SITUATION AND EXTENT.

" HERTFORDSHIRE, or Hartfordshire, is an inland
" county, bounded by Bedfordshire and Cambridge-
" shire towards the North and West, Buckinghamshire
" towards the West, Essex towards the East, and Middle-
" sex towards the South; and situated between the paral-
" lels of 51 degrees 37 minutes, and 52 degrees 5 mi-
" nutes north latitude. According to HALLEY, it con-
" tains 451,000 acres*."—It measures 28 miles from
East to West, 36 miles from North to South, and 130
miles in circumference.

SECT. II.—DIVISIONS, AND FACE OF THE COUNTRY.

THE county is divided into the eight hundreds of Odsey, Edwintree, Broadwater, Hitchin, Dacorum, Cashio,
Hertford, and Braughin. " It contains 18 market towns
" and 120 parishes*."

* Mr. WALKER.

To those, who consider picturesque beauty as an object
of pursuit and pleasure, Hertfordshire will appear deficient
in these grand scenes of Nature, in very extensive rivers,
and stupendous mountains, in those scenes which form the
beauties of Wales and Switzerland : and yet we must allow, although the features of this county are of a milder
cast, that it still contains scenes of considerable beauty :
the Southern line of the county, the heights of which
overlook Middlesex, and the hills of Surrey, is emi-
nently pleasing : the various scenes round Ware, North
Mims, Watford, and all the banks of the streams from
Berkhamsted and Hempstead, when viewed from the
adjoining hills, merit our attention ;—while, for a great
and commanding view over a rich vale, few prospects
without a great river, are more striking than that which is
seen from Lilly-Hoo.

A considerable addition is made to the beauty of this
county, by the villas and seats of rich proprietors present-
ing themselves to our view in every direction. Although
they occupy a considerable space of ground, which would
otherwise be held by common farmers ; yet their deco-
rated lawns, and ornamented grounds, not only adorn the
country, and please the traveller's eye, by their neatness
and general beauty, but may also be considered as a national benefit, from the very extensive employment with
which they supply the industrious poor in their neighbourhood.

SECT. III.—CLIMATE.

I MET with no registers of the weather ; nor would
they probably have contained any thing materially different from other counties equally southern The harvest is

not

not forwarder here than in Cambridgeshire; and in the thickest woodland parts, where the soil is wet, it is not so forward as in the more open parts of that adjacent county.

SECT. IV.—SOIL.

UNDER this head I shall first insert the notes that I took, in the order in which they occurred; and then, by a reference to the annexed Map, offer some general observations on the principal distinctions of soil in Hertfordshire.

On entering the county from Hockerill, I found at Sawbridgworth, Gilston, and Widford, clay or strong loam; but in the vales a drier loam on a gravelly bottom: here and there I saw a field of turnips, but in general, summer fallows: here is no chalk near the surface; a little may be found at Stansted and at Little Hadham. Pits have been sunk, but the quality of the chalk is not good: at Watton some is seen, and also at Saccomb; but the chalky soil properly begins at Welwyn, and continues beyond Buntingford.

In the angle of country formed by Hockerill, Ware, and Buntingford, I found the vales, and slopes descending to them, every where containing good loam on gravel and chalk, but the tops of the hills consisted invariably of strong loam, or of clay, partly wet, and partly drained.

At Little Hadham I found a strong loam, very wet, and not drained, upon a clay-marle bottom, exactly like the Suffolk loam. On this soil chalk has been tried, but without any effect, as Mr. BENJAMIN JONES, a very sensible, intelligent farmer, informed me.

From Puckeridge to Buntingford, the vale and the slopes adjoining are of a considerable breadth, and the soil of a

quality

quality superior to any, which I have yet seen in the county :—they consist of a fine, rich, deep loam on chalk. These soils are excellent ; but as the fields here are chiefly inclosed, the quantity of fallow is more extensive, than it ought to be, consistently with reason and common sense.

On the hills, as in every part where I have been, the soil is a clay, or a strong and wet loam.

About Westmill, on the hills above Mr. GREG's, I found the tenacity of the land great, and a little rain had made it like mortar; but the wheat crops shewed its fertility.

The same heavy land continues as far as Walkern, with little variation ; but towards Aston, and to Broadwater, by Stevenage, the chalk appears, where the surface is broken ; and the fields are loam, with a quantity of turnips as extensive as large tracts of open fields will permit.

Round the latter place, a poor, hungry, watery gravel, mixed with a sterile clay, abounds: the worst and most unprofitable land that I have seen in England. Some tracts of better land, however, rented at 20s. an acre, are to be found here. Hatfield, Hide, and North Mims, are specimens of the bad land abounding with blue pebbles.

Chalk is the basis of the whole county, and found universally in digging wells: it abounds at Hatfield, and occasions on the parsonage farm there a particular circumstance : a glynn about 40 feet deep, and more than an acre of land in extent, receiving, after hasty rains, the wash of Miller's-park and other lands, becomes a lake.

Much loam and turnip land lies about Watton, and along the road to Hertford; where the loam district is very apparent. On what was called the Watton estate, of 5000 acres, when possessed by the BOTELERS, great tracts of clay may be found.

In

In the vicinity of Hertford there is a tract of good dry loam; but going by Cole-green to Hatfield, I soon came to much poorer land. The manure laid on throughout the whole district sinks in two or three days by swallows, as they are called, into the chalk sub-stratum, and is lost. There is a dell similar to that which I mentioned before, at Potterils, in North Mims, where strangers, on opening their shutters in the morning, have been astonished to see a fine lake where they had been walking the day before, and seen no water. Mr. KEATE digs up the earth brought by these floods, and uses it as a manure: it may be called a *warp*; but in fertility it is far inferior to the warp of the Trent.

Some good sandy loams are seen about Astwick, which improve towards Sandridge, where, and near it, as far as St. Albans, and round that town, deep flinty loams are found on a chalk basis, and are held to be very good land. At Sandridgebury, dry gravels are mixed with light sand, and are subject to cake with rain: this sand is found on the high lands, but the lower grounds consist of good friable loams, and of clayey loams mixed with flints, an excellent soil, although hard to plough: all these are held to be good turnip land.

The similarity of soil is great from St. Albans to Watford, in Rickmersworth, and from Chesham to Berkhamsted: the whole country is under the turnip course; the loams are more or less flinty, on a chalk basis. Towards the latter place, we find a reddish clayey loam, full of flints, on the universal chalk basis; which sometimes is found at the depth of 20 feet under the surface.

The same soil continues about Hempstead and Beachwood; and the whole is by turns sown with turnips; and even that, which they call the clay, does well when sown with sainfoin.

About

About Hitchin, all is either chalk or gravel ; but chalk is found at various depths under all the country. The chalk varies from the hard sort of the beautiful downs of Lilly-Hoo, to what they call *marme* in the vales, resembling the white vale of Dunstable, but inferior. The arable lets here from 20s. to 30s. an acre, tithe free; but the average of some miles does not exceed 16s. including both soils.

About King's-Walden they have some sandy, and some strong loams, with many flints, on a chalk basis : these continue, with variations, to Welwyn ; thence to Wheathamstead and St. Albans; the whole being turnip land. At Wheathamstead they call their soil a gravelly clay, stony rather than flinty; but the word *clay*, in Hertfordshire, is every where, except in the line of country to the south-west against Middlesex, to be taken with much latitude. From St. Albans to Redburn, the soil is of an excellent quality, and superior to many named, but still partakes of the same quality. The vale to Watford, and about that place, spreads more than common, and is also very good land : it contains turnip loams, with more or less flint, on chalk. The first great change, that follows, is between Munden and Aldenham ; there the true Middlesex clay commences. This soil, a Sussex, or a Surreyman, would admit to be clay, yet would laugh at such an expression, when applied to turnip loams. It is indeed an absurdity to use the same term to mark land commonly under turnips, and that land on which they can never thrive. This clay district is of a very small extent, not more than from one to three miles in breadth.

A clear distinction of soil from any hitherto described, is met with at Cheshunt ; a very rich pale reddish sand of an admirable texture, deep, moist, and friable, yet so adhesive, as sometimes to bind. It lets at 40s. an acre, and may be consi-

considered as cheap; for it produces in favourable seasons and circumstances, five quarters of wheat an acre: it is viewed to advantage immediately out of Mr. Russel's garden. This noble vein of land continues to Hoddesdon, and to the hills before Ware. The vale is, for Hertfordshire, very wide, and is upon the whole the best land that I have seen in the county.

At Wadesmill, between Ware and Puckeridge, another sort of soil is found; a real strong clayey loam, formerly wet, but now hollow-drained, and fallowed, without flints or stones; yet in the slopes of the hills, and the vales, chalk is every where discoverable. These lands, when sown with wheat, are all in the two-bout Essex ridge. I saw no land deserving the term *red:* very little *marme,* or what may be called marle. The farmers chalk their best corn-land.

The soil of Rushden and Bradfield is clay: I was almost buried in the lanes in September. The soil of Weston is chalk on the Baldock side; the rest is stiff land. Sandon is the same. Cloth-hall, which means Clay-hill, according to CHAUNCEY, contains about 1000 acres, or a fourth of the parish, towards Baldock, on chalk; the rest is a strong wet loam, on which hollow-draining is a great improvement. Some of the chalk-land there suits turnips. The soil from Barkway to Royston is poor.

About Royston, the chalk district is clearly marked: all the soil here is a chalk; and not much of it is so good as to deserve the term of marme. The parish of Therfield is heavier and better, but is still chalk: these chalky soils Mr. FOSTER thinks by no means good turnip land; for though good crops may, by dressings, be procured, yet if the crop be not fed off very early, the barley is uncommonly liable to miss.

They

They speak of red and white land round Baldock.

At Albury, Pelhams, their neighbourhood, and about these places, this clay is still more decidedly marked. It perfectly resembles the clays adjoining in Essex, and is managed nearly in the same manner; but in all the vales and slopes still the signs of the chalk basis are seen. From Braughin to Barkway, the features change gradually as you advance; and this clay becomes some shades more white and *marmy*, indicating the approach decidedly of the pure chalk district on the northern borders of the county. These clays at Albury are far too wet and adhesive for turnips; a root which is never sown on them, as it is asserted, but with loss.

The soils traced in the Map may be termed:

1. Loam,
2. Clay,
3. Chalk,
4. Gravel.

But I should guard the reader against the idea that this is an accurate discrimination: the truth is, that the soils of this county mix and run into each other in a remarkable manner; so that, except, in the case of chalk, and that singularly unfertile land, which I term *gravel*, they are traced and named with a good deal of uncertainty; not for want, I trust, of attention in making the observations, but from the varying qualities of the respective soils.

It is necessary here to make another general and previous remark, that the quantity of stone and flint does not determine land to be gravel in this general description. Some of the best soils in the county are so flinty, that were the quantity of flints to determine to which of the above-mentioned classes they belong, they must be assigned to that of gravel; but the loam intermixed is so valuable in its nature, being dry enough to admit every advantage

arising

arising from the culture of turnips, and strong enough for wheat, that it would, with a view to its cultivation, be improperly arranged under any other head than that of loam.

OBSERVATIONS ON THE GENERAL FEATURES OF THE COUNTRY.

I every where remarked, that the vales through which the rivers and brooks flow, are composed of a rich sandy loam, with the exception of a small quantity of peat and marshy moor: that the slopes of the hills falling to these vales are inferior qualities of the same loams, and also dry and sound; but that the flatter surfaces of the higher lands are composed of a wet and strong loam, tending more or less to clay, as it is called in this county, but which is a real loam, plainly to be distinguished from the true clay marked in the Map. Much of this loam, however, is strong and wet enough to be greatly improved by hollow-drains. Few better soils are found than many of the vales of this county.

1. *Loam.*

The loams here may properly be divided into flinty and sandy; the former spread into a considerable tract from the Beane to the limits of the county beyond Berkhamsted, extending south to the gravel and clay districts, and north to the chalk: to the south of that town, towards Chesham, they are of a reddish colour, called red clay; and are strong, and in some parts tenacious, but kept loose and friable by the flints and due tillage. Some tracts, from a degree of wetness, requiring drains, are called clays, but improperly: indeed there is scarcely a more general error in various parts of the kingdom, than that of giving this term to loams of various descriptions. The district of

loam

loam in Hertfordshire is every where under a turnip course, and the crops are fed on the land; a circumstance sufficient to shew that the soil is some degrees removed from the real clay of farmers; and without any similarity to the clay of chemists, with which we have nothing to do in an agricultural inquiry. For some miles about Buntingford these loams are strong, and very fertile in wheat; from St. Albans to Redburn, and about Watford, they are a fine mellow turnip land, easily worked, and equal to the production of almost any crop. But the finest loam, that I saw in the county, is the sandy vale of Cheshunt, to Hoddesdon, &c. a distinction from all the rest of the county, it possesses adhesion without tenacity, and friability without looseness: equal to all the productions of the climate: it produces five quarters of wheat per acre; and I have every reason to conclude that it would yield 500 bushels of carrots.

2. *Clay.*

The two clay districts, as marked in the Map, are small. The southern is the most stiff, harsh, and tenacious, being the same soil as the bean lands of the north of Middlesex. The north-eastern district nearly resembles the clay lands contiguous in Essex; being rather a strong wet loam on a stiff basis of clay-marle: both, but especially the last, are in a great measure free from stone and flint, so generally abounding in the county: turnips are rarely cultivated on them, and ought never to be seen there: the latter would do well, with proper precautions, for cabbage, but that crop is unknown upon them at present *. By means of ample dressings of London manures, the southern clay is converted to very rich hay-ground, and this clearly is the most profitable application of the soil.

* Query?   H.

3. *Chalk.*

3. *Chalk.*

The Map marks the extent of this district; but chalk forms the basis at different depths of the whole county, unexceptionably; and is a great treasure, as will appear under the article of Manures. The surface chalk consists of two variations: chalk with no other mixture than what ages of cultivation and manuring have added; and what is called *marme*, which is a white marle from the mixture of a portion of clay. Both these soils are good; but the latter is the best: both are well adapted to sainfoin.

4. *Gravel.*

The district to which I give this term, is, I believe, the most unfertile that we find in the south of England; nor have I the least doubt of the superiority of the great moors in the north of England, which are to be rented for a shilling, and even sixpence per acre. I farmed this soil for nine years at North Mims, and therefore presume, that I know it well.

The characteristics of this soil are wetness, or spewiness, as the farmer terms it, from many springs; most of which are sulphury, and extremely unfriendly to vegetation, abounding more or less with smooth blue pebbles; which, at various depths, are conglomerated by sulphury clay into plumb-pudding stones, in some places so near the surface, as to impede the plough; if set for an inch or two at a greater depth than the old scratchings of bad ploughmen: it is stiff without a matrix for the roots of plants; and sharp and burning even in the immediate vicinity of springs: it has much sticky clay in the composition, but of a most sterile nature. I hollow-drained many acres;
but

but as I was obliged to employ the pick-axe, the expense
was too great ; and I found that the ploughing it into high
ridges was considerably the best way of draining it. When
it had been drained, manures had then a great effect for a
time ; but such was the voracity of the soil, that the
benefit of manuring was soon lost ; even when it had been
laid down for pasture some years, as a preparation for corn ;
the best improvement that can be made on it, when cultivated for such a purpose. It is, however, well observed
by Mr. WALKER, that this soil is best adapted to wood ;
for I was surprized to see the hedges thriving with great
luxuriance on land not worth cultivation. The district I
have marked for this miserable gravel, has many fields of
better land ; especially where any brooks or little streams
surround them ; even in North Mims, which I may call
the most sterile part of the county, even there, in the lower
parts of the parish, we find some fields of a fine mellow
friable loam, extremely valuable ; but the general feature
of the whole district is a sulphury gravel.

I have had a Map of the county carefully measured, by
which measurement it appears, that Hertfordshire contains   -   -   -   472 square miles.

chalk,	-	73
clay,	- -	141
The district of rich loam,	-	8
loam,	-	223
poor gravel,	-	27

472

The county contains, in the whole, 302,080 acres:

Of these $\left\{\begin{array}{r} 46,720 \\ 90,240 \\ 5,120 \\ 142,720 \\ 17,280 \end{array}\right\}$ acres are $\left\{\begin{array}{l} \text{chalk.} \\ \text{clay.} \\ \text{rich loam.} \\ \text{loam.} \\ \text{poor gravel.} \end{array}\right.$

302,080

SECT. V.—WATER.

" *Rivers and Streams.*—The principal rivers are the
" Lea and Colne ; and these are composed of many infe-
" rior streams, most of whose sources lie within the
" county, and join the principal rivers at different dis-
" tances from their source. The Lea rises near Lea-grave,
" in Bedfordshire, enters Hertfordshire near Bower-heath,
" and traverses the county in a direction nearly from
" north-west to south-east, to its conflux with the Stort,
" about a mile east of Hoddesdon ; then runs nearly
" south, and continues with that river, for the most part,
" the boundary of the county towards the east. The
" Maran, or Mimerum, rises near Frogmore, in Hit-
" chin hundred ; and with the Beane, which rises near
" Cromer, in Odsey hundred, joins the Lea near Hert-
" ford. The sources of the Rib are near Buntingford,
" in Edwintree hundred ; is increased in its course by
" the waters of the Quin, which rises near Biggin, in
" the same hundred, and joins the Lea between Hert-
" ford and Ware. From these rivers united, the inhabi-
" tants of the metropolis derive a leading comfort of life,

" con-

" conveyed to them by the New River. The source of
" the Ash is also in Edwintree hundred: it rises near Up-
" perwick, and falls into the Lea about a mile below
" Ware. The Stort rises in Essex; is navigable from
" Bishops Storford to its junction with the Lea, which
" is also navigable from Hertford to the Thames. Se-
" veral other small streams, whose sources are also in
" Hertfordshire, fall into the Stort, which is principally
" the eastern boundary of the county towards Essex,
" from near Bishops Storford to its junction with the
" Lea. The Verulam, Verlam, or Muse river, rises in
" Dacorum hundred, near Marget street, and the con-
" fines of Bedfordshire; runs nearly S.S.E. to St. Albans,
" and by the walls of the Roman Verulam; from
" thence nearly south, watering some meadows in its
" course, till it loses its name and consequence near
" Colney-street, in the river Colne, which is there a
" small stream, and rises near Kix, or Kits-end, in Mid-
" dlesex, taking nearly a northern course to North Mims,
" then north-west to Coney-heath, and from thence
" nearly south-west, to its conflux with the Muse, being
" joined near the conflux by a small stream which rises
" near Elstree. The classic Verulam, now under this
" name (Colne), runs nearly south-west to Watford, then
" west by south to Rickmersworth, and about a mile
" and a half beyond it, and from thence nearly south,
" till it leaves the county. The Gade, which rises also
" in Dacorum hundred, near Gaddesden, and the con-
" fines of Buckinghamshire, joins near Corner-hall the
" Bulburn river, which rises near Penley-hall in the
" same hundred, and takes from the junction nearly a
" south by east direction; runs through Lord CLAREN-
" DON's and Lord ESSEX's parks, at King's Langley and
                                            " Cashio-

" Cashiobury, and then nearly south-west to its conflux
" with the Chesham river near Rickmersworth, and to
" its junction with the Colne.

" These are the principal streams which intersect and
" water the county of Hertford in all directions; and
" they would unquestionably be of the utmost conse-
" quence (if not shackled by mill-owners) in watering
" the adjoining meadows and low grounds, in a county
" which produces so little natural grass. The Nine
" Sister springs of the celebrated Cam at Ashwell, the
" source of the Hiz near Hitchin, and the sources of
" other rivers, are in this county.

" *Canals.*—The Grand Junction canal, from Branston-
" wharf on the Coventry canal to Old Brentford, where
" it joins the Thames, enters the county of Hertford
" above Berkhamsted, and follows the course of the Bul-
" burn and Gade to Rickmersworth, and from thence
" the course of the Colne, till it leaves the county.

" The proprietors of the navigation proposed to tunnel
" under Crossley-hill, but the Earl of ESSEX, actuated
" by motives of patriotism becoming his high rank, and
" consonant with his philanthropy, agreed that the na-
" vigation should pass through his park, which it ac-
" cordingly does: great expense in tunneling was thus
" saved to the proprietors, and of freight in course to the
" public *."

An act passed for another canal from St. Albans, to
join the Grand Junction below Cashiobury-park ; but for
want of power to raise 17,000l. by subscriptions, nothing
has yet been done towards carrying it into execution.

I did not neglect inquiries into the effect which this
canal has had upon the agriculture of the county : the following minutes throw some light upon the subject.

* Mr. WALKER.

The

The summit extends four miles from Mapworth to the Cow-roast in North-Church, and is 400 feet above the level of the Thames at Brentford. The canal saves Mr. ROPER at Berkhamsted 30l. a year, in the two articles of coals and ashes.

Mr. NEWMAN HATLEY, a considerable farmer at King's Langley, has opened a trade upon the canal, in order to give him a greater command of manure for his farm. I was solicitous to know at what expense a barge could be kept constantly in employment: he favoured me with the following particulars.

The barges carry 60 tons; and their construction costs 262l. 10s. They are navigated by a bargeman and his boy, and one other man, with three horses: the bargeman and boy cost 2l. 12s. 6d. a week; the man 17s. A voyage takes ten days; locks and dues on a load of manure amount to 5l. Hay pays three farthings a mile per ton. The distance extends 25 miles. Corn and other goods, 1d¼. I was informed, that a barge-load of night-soil and sweepings of streets, in a compost, costs at London 12l.

Mr. LEACH, when the canal was first finished, brought down raw stable-dung. The whole expense of a barge of sixty tons, amounted to 20l. He manured with it five acres slightly; for a barge of sixty tons will not bring that weight of dung. It was carried away in twelve waggon-loads; and he found that this practice would not answer. Others have tried it, and all have given it up. He now confines himself to night-soil and the sweepings of streets, mixed. A barge of this will manure, in his opinion, ten acres well, and costs 20l. on the wharf. This sort is bought, and delivered in London, for 4s. per ton, into the barge, which, as he calculates, will carry sixty tons.

From

From the information which I could gain on this subject, several arrangements appear to be wanted, before this
great work can be turned to all the advantage which the
agriculture of Hertfordshire should derive from it.   It appears by the preceding notes, that the benefit of bringing
bulky manures, is extremely questionable at present ; and
the fact is, that vast quantities of hay and straw go to
London, from the very banks of the canal, by land-carriage,
the carts bringing dung back, which does not answer
when brought by the navigation.   There is an apparent
absurdity in this, which should be removed.   It seems to
arise from the want of magazines and wharfs at Padding-
ton, where a hay and straw-market should be immediately
established, so that both articles might be sold directly
from the barges, which should be immediately loaded
with manures from the wharfs.   Proper steps have not
been taken hitherto to effect these objects ; and till such
are determined, and well executed, the obvious benefits
of the work will be too speculative to effect those great
improvements which ought to result from it.   A beast
and sheep-market there should also be established, which
would prove very beneficial to all the central grazing
counties.   The preceding minutes shew that manures
come at too heavy an expense, from the double cartage
at London, which might very easily be prevented.   When
these necessary arrangements shall have been effected, we
shall see land-carriage parallel to the line of the canal laid
aside ; and a considerable saving will be made by the non-
employment of many horses ; the roads will be consequently preserved ; and the use of manures will be greatly
extended among the farmers who live within reach of the
canal.

CHAP. II.

PROPERTY.

SECT. I.—ESTATES.

PROPERTY in Hertfordshire is much divided: the vicinity of the capital; the goodness of the air and roads, and the beauty of the country, have much contributed to this circumstance, by making this county a favourite residence, and by attracting great numbers of wealthy persons to purchase land for building villas: this has multiplied estates in a manner unknown in the more distant counties. About 7000l. a-year is the largest estate in the county: there are six or seven from 3 to 4000l.; more of about 2000l.; and below that sum, of every value.

In the more eastern counties, the farmers have been very considerable purchasers of land; a circumstance that has not happened, except in very few instances, in Hertfordshire. The farms are not large, and the expenses of agriculture are higher than common; which may account for the want of this sign of farming wealth.

Freehold estates have of late sold at 28 years purchase, when any particular circumstances have not had an influence; but much of the Watton Wood-hall estate sold at 30, and some at 31, and even at 32.

SECT. II.—TENURES.

A LARGE portion of the county is held by copyhold tenure, with a fine certain, or at the will of the lord; but which fine never exceeds two years rent. Such land sells here at about six years purchase under the price of freehold.

CHAP. III.

BUILDINGS.

WERE it consistent with an agricultural work to describe the seats of the nobility and gentry; there are many, that would demand much attention: Hatfield, Cashiobury, Gorhambury, Brocket, the Hoo, the Grove, Gilstone, Ware-park, and many others, have circumstances of edifice, wood, water, or decoration, that afford matter for observation by those who travel with this object in view. I pass on to

SECT. I.—FARM-BUILDINGS.

MR. BROWN's farm-yard and offices, now building at North Mims, are the most considerable which I have seen in the county.

Mr. CASSMAJOR's barns, at North Mims, are very complete, the whole on capt stones, *consequently nearly the whole is threshing-floor, if wanted*; stacks are built at such a distance from the windows, that a cart being placed between the barn and the stack, the corn is thrown in at once, without any carting.

Mr. BAKER's barn, at Bayfordbury, is the completest of this sort which I have seen: it is very large; a threshing-floor runs over the whole, and it is covered with blue slate.

The Hon. GEO. VILLIERS, at Aldenham, has fixed

tin

tin pipes under all the eaves of the buildings round his farm-yard, for conveying away the rain that falls on them, to prevent the dung being washed by too much water. This gentleman's fatting-stalls are very wide, with conveniences for giving hay, water, and oil-cake.

The carpenter's yard of the Earl of CLARENDON, is extremely useful, and furnishes an idea of the necessary objects worthy of attention in the plan of one : these are, besides the space necessary for timber, buildings for the following purposes :

A sawing-house, and magazine for boards.

A carpenter's shop.

A nail-house.

A paint ditto, for brushes, tar and pitch, &c.

A turner's shop.

A wheeler's shop.

A wheeler's fire-house.

A magazine for fellies, spokes, &c.

Farm-yards and buildings would make a greater figure in the county, were the hay and straw not carried to London from every part of it, and were cattle a principal object of their husbandry. Attention, therefore, has not been given to this part of rural economy, so much as in more distant districts.

―――――

SECT. II.—COTTAGES.

I AM sorry not to find any minutes in my notes upon this head, which is so truly important, except the remark so often recurring, that the cottagers have no where any land, more than the small amount of insufficient gardens. I twice went out of my way to make inquiries; where I

was

was told, that one or two labourers possessed enclosed land enough to support a cow ; but the intelligence was un-founded : few labourers occupy their own cottage : upon large commons, indeed, some keep cows ; but the right goes with the cottage, which belongs to farmers or gentlemen, and consequently may at any time be taken away. The present system of supporting the labouring poor is certainly erroneous, both in practice and theory.

It appears to me as a matter of demonstration, from a multitude of facts, that the granting them land for cows, and for an ample garden, is the only cheap mode of assist-ing them materially. Wherever this system shall be fairly tried, it will speak sufficiently for itself*.

* See this subject discussed in " An Inquiry into the Propriety of applying Wastes to the better Maintenance and Support of the Poor," in 8vo. 1800 ; sold by *Richardson* and *Hatchard.*

CHAP. IV.

OCCUPATION.

SECT. I.—FARMS.

THESE are, in general, small in Hertfordshire. Not one in the county exceeds 1000 acres, and 500 form a large one; perhaps the size most common is from 150 to 400; but there are many much smaller.

The first considerable farm which I saw in the county, and one of the best conducted in it, belongs to Mr. BYDE, of Ware-park, which contains 600 acres, or about 380 arable and 220 grass. He has this year 90 acres of wheat, 84 of barley, 26 of oats, 40 of pease; in all, 240 cropped with corn; 25 of Swedish turnips, 40 of common turnips, 25 of clover, and 48 of fallow; 400 sheep, 14 horses, 7 sows and their pigs, and a good herd of Welch cattle.

Throughout the triangle of country formed by Hockerill, Ware, and Buntingford, and where the soil is generally strong, the farms are moderate; one of 400 acres is a large one; and many are very small. At the Hadhams they are even as low rented as from 20 to 30l. a-year, and the farmers are worse off than day-labourers. This part is entirely arable.

Mr. WHITTINGTON, of Broadwater in Knebworth, has a large farm well arranged, and very capitally managed. It contains 950 acres, of which 100 are grass, and 850 arable,

As

As I have noticed many particulars of the husbandry of the Marquis of SALISBURY, it will not be improper to mention, that the land to which attention is more immediately directed, consists of 290 acres in a farm, besides a park of 1050; and another, called Miller's-park, of 400, which is under wood, and in which a very extensive nursery of young oaks is carefully preserved.

About Watford, 500 acres are considered as a large farm; Mr. HATLEY at Langley, has that quantity of land.

The Duke of BRIDGEWATER's park amounts to 1080 acres; his Grace's arable to 500. He mows 400 for hay.

Mr. COTTON of Hempstead, holds 250 acres in arable, 50 in grass; he has 50 in wheat, 10 horses, 7 cows, 7 young cattle, 200 sheep.

Sir JOHN SEABRIGHT, at Beachwood, has a farm of 700 acres; he holds 300 of it in arable, 400 of it in pasture, besides 300 in wood; he has generally 300 sheep, 14 cows, and 10 to 15 stalled beasts. He cultivates 50 acres of wheat, 10 of barley, 80 of oats, 26 of pease, 5 of tares, 66 of turnips, 10 of Swedish turnips; 15 are in fallow, 32 in clover, and 2 in potatoes.

300 acres are held to be a large farm round Beachwood.

At Albury, which is a large parish, farms rise from 100 to 500 acres; in general, from 100 to 400; nor are there so many small ones of 30, 40, or 50 acres, as are common elsewhere; and the fields are large, containing 30, 40, and even 60 acres. Mr. CALVERT shewed me a rate made in the year 1667, containing 54 names of occupiers. By this it appeared, that five farms were much larger than the rest; 14 were smaller than these; the rest paid under 2s. 6d. and even as little as 2d.

About

About Royston, farms run from 250 to 700 acres. There are some small ones, of 40l. or 50l. a-year; and all these farmers are very poor, notwithstanding the high price of corn.

The parish of St. Albans, in which Gorhambury is situated, contains

16 farms of above 100l. a-year.
19   from 50l. to 100l.
17   from 20l. to 50l.
20   under 20l. and not cottages.

Lord CLARENDON holds

500 acres arable. Of these

100 are in wheat,
 70 in barley,
100 in oats,
 30 in pease,
100 in turnips,
100 in clover.

His Lordship also holds

50 of grass, which he mows. He has from
400 to 500 sheep,
 10 cows, and
 40 hogs.

Near Baldock there are are five or six large farms; Mr. Doo's, of 1000 acres, the largest in the county; Mr. Fossy, Mr. Sell, and Mr. Smith of Quickwood, hold respectively about 800.

The inquiry into the benefits of large and small farms, as a general question, belongs not to a County Report; but the vicinity to London, which influences so materially the cultivation of Hertfordshire, demands a local observation. It is the general opinion of the district, that the soil
cannot

cannot be kept in that degree of fertility necessary to support the rental and other expenses of it, without bringing large quantities of manure from the capital; a business indifferently executed on very small farms. All the exertions of this kind, which claimed any notice, are upon large ones; so much so, that I have little doubt but that the greatest breadth of land thus dressed, in proportion to the size of the farms, has been upon the two greatest in the county, though one of them, Mr. Doo's of Bygrave, is near forty miles from London; and the fact may fairly be used in argument against an indiscriminate condemnation of large farms. Another circumstance which should be noticed here is, the general predilection for the application of the sheep-fold, which is more universal in this county than in any other with which I am acquainted. What a system of waste, both of time and labour, must it be, to set a fold for 20 or 30 sheep! In proportion, therefore, as folding is necessary, a large farm is necessary; for it cannot be practised advantageously on any other.

SECT. II.—RENT.

THE BOARD, by inserting rent amongst the objects of their inquiries, have not, I apprehend, been influenced in the smallest degree by political motives. It is an object of importance in the agricultural view only of a district; and the county of Hertford affords a remarkable instance of it. The part marked *gravel* in the Map, lets at a rent which farmers could not pay, if they were not exceedingly assiduous in the purchase of manures. When rents are high, in consequence of liberal views in landlords,

lords, by assisting their tenants with long leases, with convenient buildings, by enclosing, and in various other circumstances, it is of public utility to shew and explain such liberality; and when rents are low, for want of such encouragement, of enclosures, of roads, of manures, of good breeds of live stock, or from any other cause, it is equally beneficial to mark such a result in a strong manner, as one step, at least, towards the requisite improvement.

The average of the county was not long since 12s. per acre; it is now probably 15s. according to Mr BYDE's information.

The meadows on the Stort, from Hockerill to Ware, pay from 40s. to 3l. per acre; not much is so low as 40s.

The arable in that line rents from 12s. to 16s. and some lately has been advanced to 20s. and 25s.

The rich lands about Buntingford, though open field, rent from 20s. to 21s.

Mr. BYDE's 600 acres, are at 600l. rent.

BANDOLPH's farm, part of Watton Wood-hall estate, contains 600 acres, and pays 600l.

The general rent of the county, Mr. WHITTINGTON estimated some years ago at 12s.; it is now, he thinks, probably near 15s.

Mr. ROOK calculates the rent of the county to run from 12s. to 15s.

From Barnet to Welwyn there is much lett at not more than 12s. The hungry, wet, springy gravels are mixed with a steril yellow clay, and are perhaps the worst land in England, but are improved and cultivated here by the vicinity of London. There are tracts, however, of very good sandy loam intermixed, which let at 16s. and 20s.; and much grass, which lets still higher, even to 40s.

From Hatfield to St. Albans, all round St. Albans, and

to

to Watford and Rickmersworth, the land is chiefly arable, and letts, on an average, for 20s. per acre. Grass-land is in small quantities; that which is good lets much higher.

From Chesham to Berkhamsted, Hempstead, Beach-wood, and to Dunstable, the land lets at 15s. but much at 20s. and higher.

For some miles round Hitchin the rents rise from 14s. to 16s. ; but nearer to towns, from 18s. to 25s. Almost all the land is arable ; meadow is very scarce. The butter which I tasted came from Bedford.

At Lilly, thirty years since, when Mr. Dove first went there, the averaged rent was 5s. : now it is 14s. subject to tithe.

About King's Walden, rents run from 15s. to 20s. for tithe-free land ; and from 14s. to 17s. on the road to Welwyn.

About St. Albans, the average is 18s. for tithe-free land; arable pays from 10s. to 30s. and meadows 3l. 10s.

Arable land round Watford pays from 18s. to 20s. ; about the Grove, from 8s. to 15s.

Around Rickmersworth, rents run from 12s. to 16s. per acre, subject to tithe ; pasture and meadow pay 17s.

About Munden, meadow pays 40s. ; arable, from 14s. to 7s. ; on an average 12s.

Of the southern clay district, the grass pays 40s. ; the arable 16s. From Cheshunt to Ware, the land pays 30s. ; some of it 40s.

About Albury, and the clays in the neighbourhood, 20s are paid, the lands having been advanced from 9s., 10s., and 10s. and 6d.

Seven thousand acres round Barkway, comprehending the open fields of that parish and Reed, pay 10s. per acre.

All

The open field round Royston, runs from 7s. to 10s.; the average perhaps is 9s. It would be double, if enclosed; and some of it would be treble.

The chalk country round Baldock pays from 10s. to 12s.

From these notes, which apply to every part of the county, it is clear, that the estimate of 15s. subject to tithe, for the general average of rent, is nearly the truth. Probably, the whole surface of the county included, the rent is little less.

In point of rent, therefore, it classes high amongst the English counties; much higher than the mere soil would permit, unconnected with the advantages of situation. London is a market for hay and straw to every part of the county; and manures are thence brought to every part, which, with good roads, and a general attention to the draining of most of the wet lands, and to improvements by chalking, have so ameliorated the soil, as to enable the farmer to pay perhaps 4s. per acre more rent on an average of the whole, than he would be able to do under a less favourable management.

SECT. III.—TITHE.

A COUNTRY Surveyor, acting for the Board of Agriculture, can scarcely name this subject, without some apprehension of giving offence: on one side, he is liable to be assailed by a host of writers; who seem to think, that they prove their friendship to the church by an indiscriminate condemnation of every composition that can be named for tithe; and who carry their ideas to such a length, as to attempt to shew that tithes are *beneficial* to agriculture: on the other hand, there is a race of politicians, who are as

trem-

tremblingly alive, in the same cause, from political motives.
Between the two, it is not an easy task so to treat the subject, upon any general propositions, as to be clear of mis-
apprehension and gross misrepresentation.   Fortunately, it
is not demanded of a County Reporter to treat any subject
generally ; and I shall confine myself accordingly to the
mere statement of the facts which I collected ; and I am
very happy to be able to premise, that I did not in the whole
county meet with one instance of tithes being taken in
kind ; there may be such instances in Hertfordshire, but I no
where heard of any ; and I crossed the county in so many
directions, that, if any exist, they must be extremely rare.

The following compositions are paid for the tithe in the
under-mentioned places respectively :

	Per Acre.		
	£.	s.	d.
Sawbridgworth,	0	3	0
Thundridge,	0	3	0
Ware,	0	3	0
Hadham,	0	3	0
Ditto,	0	3	0
Knebworth,	0	3	0
Datchworth,	0	5	0
Ayott,	0	5	0
Welwyn,	0	3	9
Hatfield,	0	2	0
North Mims,	0	2	6
Hempstead,	0	4	6
Flamstead,	0	3	0
Hitchin,	0	3	0
Horlwell	0	3	0
King's Walden,	0	4	0
Paul's Walden,	0	4	0

Kimpton,

				£.	s.	d.
Kimpton,	-	-	-	0	4	0
Wheathamstead,	-	-	-	0	4	6
St. Albans,	-	-	-	0	3	10
Watford,	-	-	-	0	5	0
King's Langley,	-	-	-	0	2	9
Rickmersworth,	-	-	-	0	5	0
Albury,	-	-	-	0	3	0
Barkway,	-	-	-	0	4	0
Reed,	-	-	-	0	4	0
Therfield,	-	-	-	0	3	0
Melbourne,	-	-	-	0	4	0
Bygrave,	-	-	-	0	3	6
Cloth-hall,	-	-	-	0	3	0
Average *,	-	-	-	0	3	5¼

Per Acre.

SECT. IV.—POOR-RATES.

HERTFORDSHIRE is free from any considerable manufactures, which, from depression on account of the war, or from other causes, might have left an increased population in distress; a case dreadfully experienced in the neighbouring county of Essex. It has also the advantage of being the residence of a great number of people of fortune, whose charitable attention to the poor must have operated in keeping down the poor-tax; her agriculture also affords a great and regular system of employment. The manufactures of this county are singularly beneficial,

---

* About the Grove, from 2s. 6d. to 3s. is paid. The open fields of Barkway and Reed are now commuted for one-fifth of the arable, one ninth of the grass, and one-tenth of the wood.

especially

especially that of plaiting straw, in which the earnings of the poor are very great; yet, with all these advantages, the poor-rates are high.

At Sawbridgworth the poor-rates were 3s. in the pound; they are now 12s.; and, throughout the hundred, they have doubled, on an average, in 1799.

At Ware and Thundridge, on an average of 10 years preceding 1800, they were 3s. 6d. to 4s. in the pound. In 1800, 6s.; and in 1801, 8s. 6d. At Bengeo 15s.; and at Saccomb, and Little Munden, yet more, even 16s. and 17s.

At the Hadhams they were 3s. or 4s.; and are now 12s. and 14s.

At Knebworth and Steven, they amount to 5s. in the pound; 30 years ago they were 1s. 6d.; and 10 years ago 2s.

At Hatfield they were 3s.; are now 7s.

At North Mims, 10 years ago they were 1s. 6d. to 2s.; and are now 5s.

At St. Albans they rise to 6s. notwithstanding the great earnings by plaiting straw.

At Sandridge they amount to 7s., on a rate at two-thirds of the rent.

At Bushy, the poor-rates are 2s. in the pound.

At Berkhamsted they used to be 5s. and are now 9s. in the pound; yet there are many and great charitable establishments; amongst others, a school that has 10,000l. in the public funds, where 20 boys and 10 girls are instructed: they are clothed and apprenticed out at the expense of 6l. each; and their parents have an allowance of 1s. 6d. a-week.

At Hempstead they are only 4s. and lately were but 2s. and 2s. 6d. occasioned by the very laudable exertions of three gentlemen, Mr. JENNENS, Mr. SQUIRE, and Mr. RO-
BERTS,

BERTS, who, without any expense to the parish, re-formed the work-house, which had been badly managed.

At Flamstead they have risen from 2s. to 5s.

On the calculation of three-fourths rent, they were, at King's Walden, 5s.; last year 6s.; and some years ago only 3s.

At Welwyn they rise to 7s.; were formerly 3s. 6d.

At St. Albans they were 5s. in 1800; 4s. in 1801; some years past only 2s. 6d.

At Wheathamstead they were 5s. 6d. last year.

At King's Langley they are 7s. at present, and used to run from 3s. to 3s. 6d. At Watford they rise from 2s. 6d. to 3s. 6d. At the former place they have the straw manufacture; but little of it is found at Watford.

At Rickmersworth all rates together, in 1800, amount-ed to 4s. 6d. and were formerly 2s. and 2s. 6d.

At Cheshunt they are 6s. and were 3s.

At Offley and Hitchin they were only 4s. before the times of scarcity, calculated only on three-fourths of the farmer's rent; they since amount to 8s. and even to 12s.

At Albury they rise from 12s. to 15s. calculated on three-fourths of the rent. In common times they are 5s. or 6s.

On the same calculation of rent, at Barkway they are 12s. and were 2s. 6d.

At Royston also they were 10s. and at Therfield the same.

At Bygrave they amount to 3s. on the rack-rent: they were 2s. 6d. for eight or nine years past. Formerly they were only 6d. or 9d.

The poor-rates at Cloth-hall, calculated only on three-fourths of the farmer's rent, were formerly 2s. and are now 3s. 6d.

SECT. V.——LEASES.

I AM sorry to observe, that a prejudice against the granting of leases increasing daily, will, if not checked by the good sense of the landlords, injure, beyond any calculation, the agriculture of the kingdom. Where leases are refused, let no landlord speak of bad tenants. When the lease shall cease, this effect will cease also, and there will be no longer, or at least but very seldom, any proper subject of complaint.

In that division of the county where the soil is strong, they are granted for different terms, extending from 10 to 21 years; but in the poor soil of Hatfield and its vicinity, where leases are much more necessary, none are given.

About Hitchin, the greatest part of the land is leased, for terms extending from 15 to 21 years.

But about King's Walden, although Mr. HALE gives some leases, they are not generally given.

In those of Lord GRIMSTON's tenants, for 21 years, for which term they all hold their land, I find a very inadequate, inefficient clause. It is, " that they shall not " cross-crop or sow the same land with corn above two " years together, except it be with turnips or clover, and " according to the best practice customary in the country."

To conclude this subject, about Rickmersworth and Watford, the farmers hold their land under leases for 21 years.

———————

SECT. VI.——CAPITAL, EXPENSES, PROFIT.

I INSERTED these heads, more in compliance with the commands of the Board of Agriculture, than with any idea

of

of being able to give that satisfactory intelligence relative to them on which my reader could depend. One benefit, indeed, may result from their insertion—that should any farmer be able to furnish information on any of them respectively, such information may be inserted under its proper head. I understood from one man, that on a farm of 600 acres, his expenses amounted to 4l. 9s. per acre ; but as he did not furnish me with detailed and minute calculations, I do not insert any here, that I may not unwillingly lead my reader into any error. I conceive that, in general, 5l. are necessary, per acre, in common times, for good Hertfordshire husbandry ; but Mr. Doo, of Bygrave, is clear that 7l. per acre is required, where the farmer is in the practice of buying manures.

To conclude this subject, I shall only make one or two observations more. First, that where the expenses of farming are so heavy, landlords should not be too ready to think that the rents of farms should advance rapidly with every temporary rise in the price of their produce ; and secondly, that it is by no means against the interest of farmers, that the necessary amount of their capital, and the heavy weight of their expenses, should be known

CHAP. V.

IMPLEMENTS.

PLOUGHS.— The great Hertfordshire wheel-plough is an implement in favour of which the farmers in this county are much prejudiced, and for one operation with reason—that of breaking up strong flinty fallows in a dry season. For this work of difficulty they are well calculated, from their great length of beam, sole and share, which last has a long stout point, exceedingly well calculated for making way amongst flints. I am of opinion that this plough will do such work, at times when few others would stir in such land at all. But here ends the merit; for all other works it is a heavy, ill-formed, and ill-going plough. The faults are numerous; heavier than necessary for every other work, they are all so *pitched*, that the ploughman universally walks on the unploughed land, resting nearly all his weight on the handles, his body moving in an angle of 45 degrees with the horizon. It is easy to imagine what a system of labour to the horses such a counteraction of powers must necessarily occasion; it is evident that they do labour much, even on a loose turnip soil, merely by means of the absurd construction and weight of the plough. The share, joint, and fin (which latter is placed on very backward, to enable the point to work among the stones), are at unequal levels; three or four inches of the furrow next the unploughed land, are

cut

cut three inches deeper than the rest of it ; so that when I have turned away the stirred moulds, in order to examine the unploughed land beneath, it is found all in grooves and ridges. Worse work can scarcely be imagined, while the surface is left apparently very well and neatly ploughed. Wheel-ploughs that will not go without holding, must be defective in construction. This plough will not move in its work one yard without the ploughman ; a decisive proof of its miserable construction.

Mr. Powis, at Sawbridgworth, does not approve of the great Hertfordshire plough ; he uses a smaller swing one, and very narrow in the heel, resembling more the Essex plough ; it works with two horses, and never more than with three.

Mr. Greg, at Westmill, imported Norfolk ploughs, but they would not do. After his bailiff had given me this information, I saw some bad swing-ploughs *under a shed*, with very short beams, which he called Norfolk ones ; if these only were used as Norfolk ploughs, it is no wonder that they did not succeed.

He has a double plough, with a double (not a crooked) beam, which gives satisfaction, and, as his bailiff says, is an undoubted saving ; it will not work a fallow the first time, but after one ploughing with the Hertfordshire plough, it answers well.

When I lived in Hertfordshire, the plough-shares weighed 60 or 70lb. but now about Hatfield they have reduced them to 50.

The Yorkshire plough is used by Mr. Hale and Mr. Roberts ; they even break up their land with it, using three horses, and often two.

Mr. Sedgwick approves much of the great plough, but thinks that every man ought to have the smaller one also ; a shorter beam, and a narrower furrow, for two horses.

Mr.

Mr. RUSSEL, at Cheshunt, works the Hereford swing-plough, which makes good work, and only wants a very small alteration to be an excellent tool; he was ploughing deep and clean with it, with three horses at length, and a driver.

" Hertfordshire ploughs are at least of two sorts, a
" wheel and a dray plough; I might perhaps very well
" say three or four—the small wheat-seed plough, which
" serves for sowing wheat on clean fallows, strained in by
" a man following the plough, and of course laying the
" seed under furrow, is almost peculiar to this county:
" sometimes in cross-ploughing fallows, a dray plough is
" used with a long way-tree and three horses, who will
" plough into combs or little ridges, a great deal of land in
" a day; and the harrowing these down again when
" they have lain awhile, is nearly equal to another plough-
" ing. These are perhaps the neatest and most effica-
" cious, at the same time that they are the cheapest opera-
" tions in husbandry. These three horses often go with
" long reins, and no driver besides the ploughman *."

At Albury, and the neighbouring clay parishes, and all the way to Barkway, they use the Hertfordshire foot and swing ploughs. I saw none of the great wheel-ploughs so general in the rest of the county. They use four horses in breaking up their land, but three, and even two, af-terwards.

Near thirty years ago I introduced, and used during nine years at North Mims, the same swing ploughs which I had on my farm in Suffolk: I could at that time get no Hertfordshire men to hold them, and for three or four years had all my ploughmen from Suffolk; after that, two or three of the natives were bribed to try them, and the difficulty was thus overcome. My ploughs made far bet-ter work than the common ones of the country, doing an

* MS. Anonymous.

acre

acre each per diem ; and though the expense of tillage was
thus lessened half, and the farmers admitted the work to
be well done, yet none of them attempted the same practice, saying only, that their men would never go to plough
without their horse-keeper to attend them.

Shim.—Mr. CALVERT, at Albury, has a shim that
differs from any which I have seen.

Cutting Iron.

The cutting plate, a small segment of a large circle, is
adapted to the work, which I saw it had performed in the
field, where I found it, to that of cutting up weeds on
two bout (or four furrow) Essex ridges, and of cleaning
land without ploughing or burying the soil. It dispatches
a ridge at a time; is a very good tool, and well worth attention.

I saw

I saw the same tool, but for flat work, on the farm of Mr. Doo, at Bygrave, who uses it on all occasions proper for it.

Skim Coulter.—Mr. BIGGS, near St. Albans, uses this addition, invented by Mr. DUCKET, and finds it of excellent effect in clover leys, and also whenever any rubbish is on the land that wants burying; also in breaking up a field of old sainfoin.

Chaff-Cutter.—Mr. GREG, at Westmill, has two chaff-cutters, Mr. COOK's and Mr. SALMON's; and the account which his bailiff gave me was, that the former cut it finer, and that the latter did most work. All the stock that eat hay or straw have it given in chaff.

Mr. ROOK, at Bengeo, has 400 sheep, 20 horses, and 8 or 10 cows, fed with chaff cut by a horse machine, which cuts a load of clover hay, and one quarter of a load of straw, in six hours.

Lady MELBOURNE has one of SALMON's Woburn chaff-cutters, which is turned by a horse, and a machine for bruising oats or beans, &c. being attached, both are worked at the same time; 20 bushels of chaff being, in that case, cut per hour.

Threshing-Mill.—Mr. GREG, of Westmill, has a four-horse threshing-mill, built by Mr. PITT, of Hertford; but it has not worked in any manner to his satisfaction, even for wheat, the only grain tried, and which these mills usually thresh very well. He has threshed, however, 90 bushels a-day, at the following expense:

A driver,

			£.	s.	d.
A driver,	-	-	-	0	0	7
A feeder,	-	-	-	0	1	8
A woman to supply the feeder,		-	0	1	0
A ditto to untie bands,		-	-	0	1	0
Two men to clear away the straw,		-	0	3	4
Five women at the straw,	-	-	0	5	0
Four horses, suppose	-	-	0	10	0

$$£. 1 \quad 2 \quad 7$$

But the work was not done clean. I found the drum-wheel broken to pieces, and only the beaters remaining. The draft-arms appeared to be too short, from the smallness of the building—a barn; and the dressing-machine not so fixed as to receive corn from the mill.

Mr. ROOK, at Bengeo, has a mill which works with two horses; he finds the horses, and gives the men 1s. a load, of five bushels, for threshing wheat.

Mr. BLINDEL, of Welwyn, has a mill for four horses, built by Mr. PITT, of Hertford, which in a *long* day would thresh, when in order, 10 loads of wheat, or 15 of pease; the only grain or pulse with which he has tried it. It cost about 100l. Mr. BLINDEL does not approve of it, and has not used it for the two last crops. He does not think these mills deserve attention, unless there was a certainty of their answering, and that the straw was not for sale. The arms by which the horses draw, appear to be much too short, occasioned by the want of space in the barn in which the whole is built. The drum, &c. is fixed also too low, so that no attention can be paid to catch the grain thrown out with the straw. The drum also is not closed, by which it appears that the mechanic

knows

knows nothing of the system of friction against a cover for the clean threshing of barley.

Mr. Doo, of Bygrave, has one of the most complete that I have any where seen, built by Messrs. BURN and M'DONALD, who are at present in partnership with Mr. KIER, in his patent axletrees, at Pancras. It grinds wheat, cuts chaff, and dresses the corn, and will do all these at the same time, with six horses. When it threshes corn only, its common day's work amounts from 25 to 30 loads of wheat, or to 15 quarters of barley; and it then requires two men and five women. Mr. Doo has had it four years; the repairs have been very trifling. The expense of erecting it amounted nearly to 400l. He uses it constantly, except for the wheat, the straw of which he carries to London.

Turnip-Slicer.—Mr. KEATE, of Hatfield, has a very simple and effective turnip-slicer, which cuts in common a bushel of Swedish turnips in a minute; three bushels in two minutes have been done. It is made by a wheel-wright at Hatfield, and has much merit. It cost 2l. 12s. 6d.

Scuffler.—The first scuffler which I saw in the county, was at the Rev. Mr. KEATE's, at Hatfield, made by HAND-FORD, near Loughborough, in Leicestershire; a very useful and effective tool, far more powerful than a great break, or four-horse harrow, which was now laid by in the barn as useless. This year a very bad plant of clover had been once ploughed, and this scuffler having passed once across it, I found the land in very fine order; and had it fortunately been ploughed into lands small enough to lay dry in winter, the wheat might have been better put in without more ploughing than with it. A hint others should take, that when they plough for some future

crop,

crop, so to lay their lands, that all successive ploughings may be saved, and the scuffler trusted to for a better tillage than can be given by the plough. It costs 8l. 8s.

Oil-cake Mill.—The Honourable Mr. VILLIERS has at Aldenham, a roller turning under a hopper, with stout teeth, for breaking oil-cake, in order to feed beasts, which answers its purpose well.

CHAP. VI.

ENCLOSING.

MR. WHITTINGTON calculates the difference between the rent of open-fields and enclosures, supposing the soil the same, to be about 5s. per acre.

In the enclosure of Hartingfordbury, a plan was formed to escape the charges (so often very heavy) which are made by commissioners; that of naming in the bill three neighbouring gentlemen for commissioners: Mr. BYDE, of Ware-park, Mr. NICHOLSON CALVERT, and the Rev. Mr. BROWNE. By this mode, no other expense is incurred than is absolutely necessary; these gentlemen, of course, taking nothing, but acting as friends to the parties. If this plan could be more commonly pursued, which surely it might be, enclosing would not be so much complained of.

In new enclosures, Mr. IRONS, of Market-street, banks double quicks and rails, and cleans for eight years, when he engages to deliver up a complete fence, taking his rails away, for 10s. a rod. This is a valuable fact; for it forms a fair estimate of expense in calculations of the profit and loss of new improvements.

CHESHUNT.—In this parish, the act of enclosure passed in 1799, operates on 1497 acres of common-fields and meadows, and 1168 acres of common; on 2665 acres collectively. Before enclosing, the open-fields were in the course of,

1. Fallow.

1. Fallow.
2. Wheat.
3. Spring corn; except about 100 acres, too poor for yielding wheat.

The whole parish contains	8452 acres.
Of freehold, - - -	5729
Of copyhold, - -	1083
Of lanes, commons, and marshes, -	1640
All of which, with some smaller portions,	———
make up - -	8452 acres.

By the enclosure, 86 acres are allotted for rectorial tithe of the common, and 167 for vicarial; and 100 acres are left, by direction of the act, as a stinted common for cottagers of 6l. a year and under, being vested in trust in the lord of the manor, vicar, and churchwardens. The improvement is likely to be very great; for the common was not fed by the poor, but by a parcel of jobbers, who hired cottages, that they might eat up the whole. The soil is a loamy clay, with some gravel and marsh. It has been cropped but once, having been ploughed once for oats, without any other difficulty than the cutting of ant-hills, as no grubbing was necessary. The crop was very large; of seven or eight quarters on an acre. No land was pared and burnt for that grain, but some was for wheat; and the whole was let at 20s. per acre. There is chalk under it, a soft sort, at the depth of nearly 20 feet; and a harder for lime, at 60 feet. But little of the land formerly arable, and then unenclosed, is suited for laying down to grass; we find not 50 acres in 500.

The Marquis of SALISBURY has 320 acres of copse here also.

KENSWORTH—Was inclosed in 1798: by the act, 440

440 acres of waste land were brought into cultivation, and 600 acres of open-field arable allotted. Great complaints are made of the expense of this enclosure, which are said to be uncommonly heavy.

PEMBRIDGE.—An act passed in 1780 to enclose about 176 acres of brush-wood common in this parish; but the effect was not the entire cultivation even of that small quantity.

ELSTREE.—By an act which passed in 1776, 750 acres of common were enclosed.

NORTON.—By an act of 1796, 1400 acres were enclosed; 1000 of open arable field, and 400 of common; by which a great improvement has been made; but the number of cows has decreased one-half, while that of sheep has increased one-third.

HITCHIN.—By an act which passed in 1766, 881 acres of common-field land were enclosed in this parish; part of it was clay, which has ever since been cultivated as it was before, with two crops and a fallow: but the drier part is under the turnip husbandry. The parish contains 4865 acres tithable, besides 600 acres more not tithable, as having formerly belonged to the Knights Templars.

OFFLEY.—In 1768 an act passed, by which 217 acres of common fields were enclosed in this parish, since which the cultivation has greatly improved.

LILLY.—By an act passed in 1768, an enclosure took place of 951 acres of common fields, without any commutation for tithe: it is now considered as having been a very

bene-

beneficial measure, considerably increasing the produce of the parish.

ICKLEFORD.—By an act which passed in 1776, 568 acres of common field land, and 40 of common grass, were enclosed. The parish think that their produce has been increased very little in consequence of the enclosure.

NORTH-MIMS.—By an act passed in 1778, about 700 acres of common were enclosed; but the soil was so miserably poor, being a hungry springy gravel, mixed with steril clay, that the produce has depended entirely on manuring from London, or from other lands. Much has been laid down to grass, and a small quantity planted, which may answer in the end better than any of the rest.

TRING.—In 1797 an act passed for enclosing this parish, amounting to 3533 acres, the greater part of which consists of open arable fields; some of the parish is common meadow, and 750 acres of it are common heath and furze land. The improvement is not yet finished; but in the lower grounds, part of which is fenny, it will be very great.

BARKWAY and READ.—Barkway contains 6000 acres, and Read 1000; all was under the course of two crops and a fallow, and paid a rent of ten shillings, and for tithe four shillings per acre; the commissioners' valuation amounts to eighteen shillings per acre, tithe-free. In the act of enclosure which passed last year, one-fifth of the arable, one-ninth of the grass, and one-tenth of the wood, were given; and the lord of the manor also received one twentieth. They only allot in severalty, and fence the tithe allotments; other

fencing

fencing and subdivisions are left to individuals. The improvement is expected to be very great, and that a course of turnips, barley, clover, and wheat, will be pursued by good farmers. Oats are added only by bad ones. It is conceived also, that the land will produce a load of wheat per acre more than at present. Three flocks of 1200 sheep now feed both parishes; the number may not increase, perhaps it may be less; but no doubt is entertained that more mutton and wool will be produced. The system will be, to buy in for fatting on turnips; but on which it was remarked by Mr. HOGG, that while enclosures were multiplying, as at present, and lessening every where the *breed* of sheep, it would be good policy to keep breeding flocks wherever possible; for the demand must certainly keep up the prices of store sheep.

Mr. FORSTER, a gentleman very intelligent in husbandry, at Royston *, lamented the great inconvenience of open-fields, pleading strenuously for a general enclosure. He cannot sow turnips in the open-field without leave from the parish flock-master, and pays 1s. 6d. an acre to the shepherd for not eating the crop, as there are scarcely any sheep kept but on the parochial flock-farms; and on their chalky lands they are bound by the common course, to fallow land to which much ploughing is injurious to a very great degree, making that lighter which is too light already. Most of their straw they are at present forced to send to inns, to take the dung, whereas, if the lands were enclosed, it would be more profitable for the farmers to have stock of their own.

The preceding cases are sufficient to shew that enclosing has gone on as well in Hertfordshire as we have any reason to expect in a county so generally enclosed *of old time.*

* I called also on Mr. WITHAM and Mr. PHILIPS, but found neither of them at home.

There,

There remains, however, much to be done in the northern part of the county; and there are smaller scattered common-fields in many other parts, with extensive commons also in the western district. Many of these are too small to pay the expense of a distinct act of enclosure; but all would be properly cultivated under the sanction of a general act.

FENCES.

HERTFORDSHIRE may be considered as the county where the plashing system is carried on to the greatest extent: it has been universally practised here from time immemorial. Scarcely can any county be worse situated for coals; and the copses are not more extensive than common. These causes may have induced the farmers to fill the old hedges every where with oak, ash, sallow, and with all sorts of plants more generally calculated for fuel than fences, and which would form no kind of fence under any management but their own. Here they form a material object in the rural economy of the farm, supplying the house with wood sufficient for its consumption. It evidently appears that plashing is understood and practised uncommonly well, from the circumstance of the hedges being in many parts of the county, not only fences, but good fences, when tolerably preserved, without the aid of any ditches; for I did not see a thorough good ditch (such as would be called a ditch in Suffolk), in the county, except some that I made 30 years since myself, and which may still be seen.

Whenever new enclosures are made, white-thorn

HERTS.] should

should be the only plant used ; but where the country is already enclosed with other plants, a prudent man will think twice, before he will put himself to the enormous expense of grubbing up all the old fences of a farm, and re-planting them in new lines. In common undertakings, such a thing is quite impracticable ; nor would it answer, however plentiful money might be.

For this reason, it is necessary the more fully to explain the Hertfordshire system. We have the same hedges in Suffolk, but on a soil not so congenial to the growth of wood, and under a very inferior management ; under that of cutting up all the live wood, and trusting the defence of the young growth to a dead hedge, which is presently weighed down by snow, and carried away by the poor people.

Where there are ditches, small or great, the hedge is on the top of the bank ; which is far preferable to the Suffolk method of making them on the level of the field, with an immense bank of earth *upon* the roots. When planted on this level, the Leicestershire custom is preferable, that of setting the hedge on one side of the ditch, and making the bank on the other.

Plate I. represents a winter view of a Hertfordshire hedge not plashed, of the growth of 12 years.

Plate II. represents the same hedge, with much of the growth cut out, in order for the following operations : In clearing away so much as is here represented, care is taken to leave as large a proportion of white-thorn, as may be, provided they shall be tall, large, well-grown plants.

In *Plate* III. is seen a part of the stems, left in the preceding plate, cut off for hedge-stakes. This is a part of the business, to which a good workman particularly attends ; for the strength of the hedge depends on the stakes being alive, and not dead, as used in so many counties.

I have

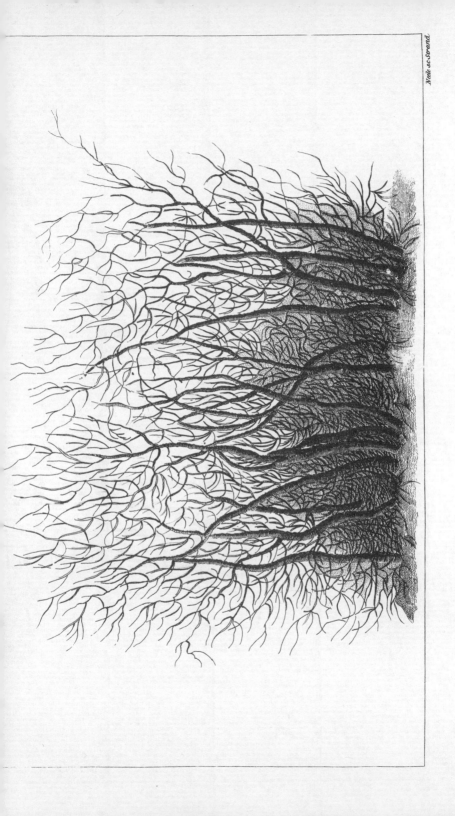

Plate II.

Plate III. Page 50

Plate IV.

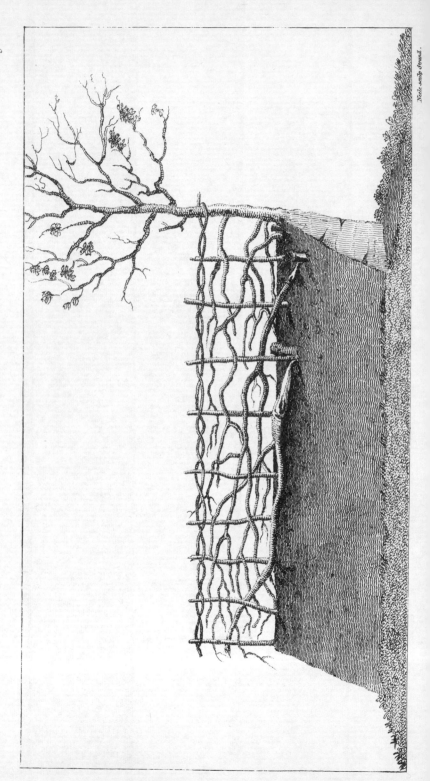

Plate VI.

Neile sculp Strand.

I have long remarked in Suffolk, and elsewhere, that when stakes are all dead, they presently rot and break; are easily pulled up by sportsmen; and then the least weight of snow, or any less accident, demolishes at once whole perches of the fence. One live hedge-stake, at least, to every three or four feet, should be left.

When necessity obliges a farmer to submit to a dead hedge, it would last four times as long, if he took care to use only sallow or willow truncheons, or, for want of them, young trees: the hedge would be greatly preserved by such stakes. The plate represents a ditch as well as a hedge; by which addition the fence is rendered complete.

Plate IV. represents the hedge in its next state: the standards are plashed down, and interwoven among the hedge-stakes; and edders * are added along the top, to keep the straggling branches in their place, and bind the whole together.

To explain the operation of plashing, a figure is added in *Plate* II. in which a large bough is plashed in the right manner. The principal caution should be, to prevent the branch from splitting: hence it is better to leave the stem united to the stump by a very thin slice, a little more than the mere bark. When it is left thick, there will be an elastic force in the branch, and it will not rest at ease in its position in the hedge: it then never thrives well, having a constant springing tendency to rise; but when it holds by a very thin piece, the wound soon gains an edging of bark, and the growth is scarcely retarded.

All the plashes are usually bent one way; but when a place in the hedge is deficient in live wood, then they may be turned to it from both sides (see *Plate* V.); in

---

* Small twigs, called in the North of England, bendings.

which

which the plash *a* is turned one way, and *b* another: in this instance, from the short space between *a* and the gate. It also shews a tree used as a hedge-stake, the edders *c c* entwining it.

Plate VI. shews the back of the bank, rounded up regularly to the hedge. Farmers who are not *neat*, leave this earth as it is thrown out of the ditch, which is a slovenly practice, covering much of the border, and at the same time leaving a gradual slope, inviting to cattle.

When the business is thus far advanced, the farmer has it in his power to manage his hedge in two ways—by the common growth, renewable for fuel every 12 years, where white-thorn is deficient; but where the plant abounds, he has it in his power, if he pleases, by clipping, to keep the fence always as represented in *Plate* VII. But let it be remembered, that such management is mere luxury and ornament, and has nothing profitable to recommend it. Hedges thus cease to be the collieries of a country.

At 12 years growth, usually, the hedge is renewed by a new plashing; when old plashed branches are cut off close to the ground, and new ones laid down. However, in some cases, where there would be gaps, for want of a live growth, these old plashes are left across, and give much strength to such places; and I have seen instances, in which a single stem has been laid across some gap, and grew past another beyond it, having the effect of a live rail many feet long, with strong perpendicular shoots from it, which, when cut off at two feet, left a range of stakes, converted to an excellent hedge by weaving in a few younger plashes.

It should in general be observed, that plashes should always be cut as close to the ground as possible; a circumstance not sufficiently attended to in the drawings.

These

These hedges, when well plashed and grown, must rival, I should imagine, the horn-beam ones, which Mr. HARTE admired so much in Germany *.

But while I give the praise which I conceive to be due in an old enclosed country, to the Hertfordshire system, it should not be concealed, that I have met with some persons who disapprove of the whole business, and prefer cutting up, as in Suffolk, &c. all the growth of a hedge on repairing it. I have also met with various remarks on the superiority of white thorn hedges. The latter assertion has nothing to do with the inquiry, since it is the management of old hedges, and not planting new ones, that is in question. I can only say, that I have had long experience on my own farms of both methods, and am perfectly satisfied of the superiority of plashing. No practice can command every suffrage; there will on all subjects be a diversity of opinion. To attempt to induce every man to think the same in farming, would be as hopeless a task as a similar endeavour in politics, or in any other subject.

Mr. BYDE weeds his hedges and borders twice a year, to free them from thistles, and whatever plants are likely to spread their seeds into the fields †.

The plashing of hedges is, as I said before, universal: they do not attempt it on hedges under nine years growth, nor when they are older than twelve; 6d. per rod is paid; where a small ditch is made, 8d. and for a few, 1s.

About Langley Bury, like other parts of the county, we meet with live plashed hedges, but which are so badly looked after, that they prove little or no security against the cattle and sheep, which are to a disgraceful degree kept

---

* Essays on Husbandry, p. 114.

† I think it highly proper to take notice in this place, of the very slovenly manner in which thistles are suffered to grow on the borders of ponds, in many counties.

in

in the lanes for three or four months in the year. Mr. KINGSMAN has found it very beneficial to add ditches three feet wide and three deep: he lays the earth to the hedges, forming thereby banks, that support them, and at the same time cut off springs, to which that part of the county is very subject.

Mr. PARKER, at Munden, approving of no plant in hedges but white-thorn, weeds out all others, and by making ditches, and by attending very carefully to nurse up the white-thorns, he gradually brings them to the state desired; whatever he cuts out, he leaves to rot in the ditch, which, with the mowings of a very narrow border swept also into it, renders the scourings of the ditches, after some years, a rich manure.

CHAP. VII.

ARABLE LAND.

WE are here come to the great object of the Hert-fordshire husbandry. By far the greatest part of the county is under tillage, for which the county was singularly famous perhaps before the improvements in Norfolk were began; and it may not be improper to observe, before I enter on the particulars to be detailed here, that there are two opinions relative to the progress of husbandry in this county. Thirty years ago, when I resided in it, I often heard the Duke of LEEDS remark, that the Hertfordshire farmers, through the period of his recollection (and he was an old man), had stood *still*, at least; perhaps had declined in the merit of their agriculture; and this appears from the writings of ELLIS, who lived in this county, and whose books were published from 60 to 75 years since. There are at present scarcely any practices to be met with in the county, that were not well understood at that period.

Mr. ROOPER, of Berkhamsted, informs me, that turnips and clover are supposed to have been introduced into this county in the time of OLIVER CROMWELL, who gave 100l. a year on that account to a farmer of the name of HOWE. It appears also by old leases, that the course of crops, and the management in general, have experienced very little change in the last hundred years.

Clover was introduced between 50 and 60 years ago at Dunstable.

Mr.

Mr. SEDGWICK, of Rickmersworth, has known the county well for 27 years, and is clear, that it is much improved: they fallow less for wheat, and sow more turnips and clover; they also manure and plough better.

Possibly both these opinions may have truth in them. In the great features of management, the agriculture may be nearly the same; yet, in some particulars, additional energy may have been exerted.

SECT. I.—TILLAGE.

THE variations found in different countries, in the operations of tillage, are much deserving attention; for though a single county may not afford intelligence, which, separately considered, appears to be of much importance; yet when the whole kingdom comes to be examined and reported, and the circumstances compared and combined, as soils may require, a considerable degree of light may be thrown on the subject. The Hertfordshire farmers have an idea of their great perfection in this branch of their business; but I do not conceive, that others will be very ready to allow it.

Ploughing.—On my reporting to Mr. BYDE, of Ware-Park, the bet made between Sir JOHN SEBRIGHT and Mr. COKE, he carried me to one of his strong-soiled fields, which had been a clover ley ploughed once in dry weather in June, as a sample of tillage, which he conceived impossible to be effected with two horses; and remarked, that on this stiff land, one such earth, in dry roasting weather, does more good than several, when the land works easier; but as to touching it when moist, it is pernicious; even

the

the great Hertfordshire plough wanted a stone of 50 or 60 pounds weight in its body, to keep it steady.

The common depth of ploughing about Westmill, is four or five inches; but Mr. GREG ploughs as deep as the staple will admit; which account of his bailiff implies, that five inches are not the depth of the staple. The crops in that vicinity are so great, that I should suppose there cannot be any material error in the basis of their practice.

Mr. WHITTINGTON remarks, that winter tillage is but of little use; he avoids it as much as possible; and has found that the application of a *break*, or a large four-horse harrow, is a good substitute for some ploughing.

The price of ploughing about Hatfield, amounts to 11s. and 12s. an acre; twenty years ago, 7s. were paid; all is done with four horses and a driver; 20s. per acre have been paid in the new enclosure at Cheshunt.

In the 17 acres of experiment ground of the Marchioness of SALISBURY, the cultivation was began by a powerful trench ploughing, 18 inches deep. Mr. STEPHENSON, the manager, who, having been head gardener, had the farmer's best education, knew that her Ladyship intended to cultivate parsnips, carrots, cabbages, and other plants demanding deep tillage, and very wisely began on garden principles. He remarks, that in general, in Hertfordshire, there is a deficiency in not ploughing to a greater depth; they have a prejudice against it, and think land ruined that is stirred deeper than common : it is admitted that the first crop will sometimes suffer in spots, but the succeeding ones make ample amends. Barley has been sown on trench ploughing, and with success; in a dry season it grew well, while that for which the land had been differently prepared, stood still.

Mr. PRATCHET, of Hatfield, having asserted that he would readily give for ploughing his land once over, 12s.

per

per acre, and that he was sure it cost him more, I re-
quested the particulars on which he founded his opinion:
his calculations are as under:

	£.	s.	d.
Four horses, seven bushels oats, at 4s.	1	8	0
Eight trusses of hay, at 5l. - -	1	2	2
Ploughman, - -	0	15	0
Driver, - - -	0	12	0
Wear and tear, plough and harness,	0	6	0
	£ 4	3	2

They plough five roods per day, when they break up
their land, and one acre and a half when they give it a
second, or any subsequent ploughing.

At seven acres and a half per week, the expense amounts
to 11s. and 1d. per acre, besides the wear of the horses.

At nine acres, it amounts to 9s. 2½d.; but the above
estimate of Mr. PRATCHET is drawn from the consideration, that this includes none of the time when the horses
are unemployed, which is a very material point, and adds
largely to the expense when they work; on a wet-land
farm particularly, the time thus lost is considerable.

Mr. DEARMAN, of Astwick, speaking of ploughs, remarked, that the great wheel-plough did well in summer;
for although the horses were harnessed abreast, they did
no harm; but in winter they poached and injured the land.
The foot-plough is used with three horses, one before, and
another walking in the furrow. This observation is certainly just.

Mr. COOK, from near Colchester, in Essex, bailiff to
the Duke of BRIDGEWATER, is of opinion (however prejudiced in favour of two-horse ploughs), that they could
not break up for a fallow the flinty clayey loams of this
country,

country, but that after one ploughing, they are fully equal to the following tillage.

In every part of Hertfordshire they have a method of ploughing, of which they are very fond, called combing, or hacking: a field that lies on flat or broad lands, is half ploughed across, by beginning with a furrow and returning; the plough doubles the breadth of it by a second furrow, the contrary way *from* the former, leaving a very small baulk, just sufficient to give steadiness to the plough, by a purchase against unstirred land, which is equally well effected by leaving no baulk, but by going two inches deeper on the land side. Then the plough returning for the third time, throws back the last turned furrow, taking up earth enough under it to clean plough the whole land, if wanted, or to do it at such spaces as to whole plough, or half plough the field; but if combed close, the surface is left in regular narrow ridges, called combs. This operation, with a little difference in the execution, is called *ribbling* in Suffolk. It prepares a good hold for the harrows. I saw it well executed at Sir JOHN SEBRIGHT's, at Beachwood, who understands the Hertfordshire tillage well.

Bouting, as it is called, is the lapping of two furrows together, by forming narrow ridges, a *bout* in each; then they are reversed in the same manner by splitting; after that, they plough down by one furrow in the centre of each ridge, and so leave it for harrowing: some time elapses between each operation. In breaking up, they do an acre a day, sometimes more.

About Hitchin, they break up with the common Hertfordshire plough; but in stirring, use the swing-plough with three horses, and sometimes with two.

At Mortgrave, near Hitchin, Mr. GREEN is settled, who came from near Clare, in Suffolk, about four years ago.

ago. He never uses more than two horses in a plough, and does his work just as well as the natives with four: he succeeds, and is supposed to be a very thriving man. Some of his Suffolk ideas, however, are said not to have answered so well, particularly the making composts with ditch earth : this he has given up, and now goes to London for manure, like others.

Mr. SEDGWICK recommends, in ploughing broad lands with the common plough, to leave two or four furrows for the small narrow plough, to finish the lands, by which means there are channels on the slopes of the open thorough to catch seed; whereas, with the great plough, the seed rolls into those thoroughs.

Mr. PARKER, of Munden, uses the foot-plough of Middlesex, as preferable to the great Hertfordshire wheel-plough, and can break up flinty strong land with it as well as the other performs it : cases very rarely happen, in which the country plough has the advantage. He has a great opinion of deep ploughing; never has the least objection to any depth, nor ever yet checked his men for going too deep. His common depth is nine inches. This he has practised 23 years on good loamy land in Huntingdonshire, and here, on the gravels and flints of Hertfordshire. He has never lost a crop by it, but met with an unvarying success; and is clearly of opinion, that at this time of day it ought not to be made a question, but received as an admitted fact. He does not limit his ploughs to nine inches, for he would like twelve better, if easily attainable.

He has no idea of *burying* dung, but ploughs it in nine inches deep, and would plough it in deeper; for he is well assured from experience, that nothing is lost; and a great advantage of depth is, that one ploughing given deeply and clean, is of more effect and better than two, or even than

ten,

ten, such scratchings as are called ploughing often in this country; but the harrows, in *cleaning*, should, upon loamy soil, be as deep as the ploughing.

At Albury, &c. on their clays retentive of moisture, they are extremely attentive never to go on in wet weather. The soil is stiff and ticklish, and, if touched when too moist, is greatly injured. The fact is general.

Mr. KING, of Barkway, who has *Suffolk* connexions, ploughs with a pair of horses, and no driver; and does as much, and as well, as his neighbours with four.

Harrowing.—Mr. GREG, at Westmill, uses a very stout four-horse harrow on some occasions, to save ploughing. A crop of winter tares failing, he thus worked the land for barley, without ploughing. I saw the crop, and it promises six quarters an acre. Mr. WHITTINGTON uses this machine also, and finds it, on some occasions, preferable to ploughing. In above 100 miles, I have neither found nor heard of any scuffler, a tool so essential in good management.

SECT. II.—FALLOWING.

UNDER this head I am happy to have but a word to insert—The fallow system, except in a very small district, and in open fields, is not much pursued in this county. Wherever turnips can be sown, we find them; and consequently fallows, in a county containing but little real clay, are confined, as they ought to be, to the most difficult and impracticable soils. The observation must not, however, be taken as universal; for in every part of the county they accidentally take place, when land is got, by

ill

ill management, so foul as to make a complete fallow more advisable than turnips, as the means of cleaning it.

"While weeds continue to grow and increase in the
"best cultivated lands, fallowing will be practised in
"Hertfordshire and elsewhere, where farming is under-
"stood, till a substitute less expensive, and equally suc-
"cessful, in destroying weeds, is discovered. Here the
"fallows generally succeed the crops of oats, and are
"thus made: the land is ploughed up in the autumn, to
"be mellowed by the winter frosts, and lies in that state
"till the Lent corn is sown in the succeeding spring; it
"is then ploughed again, and, if full of couch and black
"grass, torn to pieces with harrows, and the couch, &c.
"collected in heaps, and burnt; it then remains untouch-
"ed, till the seeds of the weeds therein, or the greatest
"part of them, have vegetated; when it is ploughed
"again, and harrowed, if necessary, and the season will
"permit, and the remaining couch collected and burnt.
"The last ploughing is the most important, and should
"be made a short time before the crop of wheat is sown,
"when all the remaining seeds of weeds have vegetated,
"and before any of them have seeded; the grain then
"sown and well harrowed in, will have the start of the
"weeds, thus as much destroyed as possible; and a spring-
"dressing, if necessary, will enable it to keep them effec-
"tually under. Fallowing thus made in favourable sea-
"sons, renders fallowing in future less necessary *."

* Original Report.

SECT. III.—COURSE OF CROPS.

THE more attention any agriculturist may give to this subject during a long series of experience, the more importance he will attach to it. The bad husbandry met with in so many districts of the kingdom, arises from a want of knowledge in this point, more than from any other defect.

In the clays and strong loams of Sawbridgworth, we find the under-mentioned course of crops:

1. Fallow,
2. Barley,
3. Clover,
4. Wheat;

also,

1. Fallow,
2. Barley,
3. Pease,
4. Wheat.

Mr. PARRIS, of the parsonage-farm, shewed me a field of very fine wheat; part under the first of these courses, and part under the last; both very good; but the stubble was cleanest on the clover part.

Mr. PLUMER, M. P. for the county, has some of his fields in,

1. Fallow,
2. Wheat,
3. Fallow,
4. Barley;

and he assured me that many farmers pursue, on a part of their lands, the same course:

1. Fallow,
2. Wheat,

3. Fallow,

3. Fallow,
4. Barley,
5. Clover,
6. Oats.

Whatever fault may be found, and perhaps justly, with so much fallowing, it must be admitted that their crops are good.

Mr. BYDE, of Ware-Park, whose farm chiefly consists of strong land, makes it an unvarying rule, never to take two crops of white corn running, on any account whatever.

All the turnip-land Mr. BYDE knows in the county of Hertford, is thus managed:

1. Turnips,
2. Barley,
3. Clover; the first crop mown, the second fed.
4. Wheat;

good farmers stopping here, and bad ones adding,

5. Oats.

The turnips may be reckoned at 50s. an acre; the barley three quarters, and the wheat 17 to 20 bushels.

Upon the strong heavy soils they crop their land almost equally, in general, as under:

1. Fallow,
2. Wheat,
3. Fallow,
4. Barley,
5. Clover,
6. Oats;

and vary their course thus:

1. Fallow,
2. Wheat,
3. Clover,

4. Barley,

4. Barley,

5. Fallow,

6. Wheat,

7. Oats, pease, or beans.

An acre of wheat yields 25 bushels.

But about Watford, he informs me there is a peculiar course of,

1. Fallow,

2. Beans, on which they put all the dressing,

3. Wheat.

At Little Hadham, on the strong land, there is a course of,

1. Fallow, ploughed four times,

2. Wheat,

3. Fallow, four or five times ploughed,

4. Barley;

the only variation, sometimes adding,

5. Clover,

6. Oats;

but Mr. JONES is decidedly of opinion, that the crop and fallow course is the most profitable. He *asserts*, that beans will not succeed on this soil. I *know* they will on land exactly such in Suffolk, and give four quarters per acre.

Mr. GREG's farm, at Westmill, is in a course of,

1. Fallow, ploughed four times,

2. Wheat,

3. Clover,

4. Barley, on three earths,

5. Pease;

and this course is not uncommon amongst the farmers.

Mr. WHITTINGTON, on light land, cultivates,

1. Turnips,

2. Barley,

3. Clover,

HERTS.]   4. Wheat;

    4. Wheat ; and if the land is in good order, he adds,

    5. Pease, or oats.

On clay land, his course is,

    1. Fallow,

    2. Wheat,

    3. Pease ;

or,

    1. Fallow,

    2. Barley,

    3. Pease ;

or,

    1. Fallow,

    2. Wheat,

    3. Clover,

    4. Oats ;

and this he reckons better than either of the former.

I proposed barley on a fallow with clover, and then beans and wheat ; but he objects, that if clover is sown at the time of sowing barley, it gets so forward, as to spoil the crop ; and if sown at rolling, it is apt to fail. This I cannot admit to be fair reasoning, in a country where it is common to sow clover on wheat in the spring, and even so late as May and June.

The Marchioness of SALISBURY, and the Rev. Mr. KEATE, are both in the course of,

    1. Turnips,

    2. Barley,

    3. Clover,

    4. Wheat.

But clover is very apt to fail ; in which case her Ladyship sows spring tares. Mr. KEATE fallows. The lady is here the better farmer.

Much poor hungry gravel in the open-fields near Hatfield, let at 7s. per acre, in which the rotation is,

    1. Fallow,

1. Fallow,
2. Wheat, producing two or three loads *
3. Oats; produce 2½, or three quarters.

On better land, enclosed, they cultivate,

1. Turnips, sheep-fed;
2. Barley; four quarters are produced, on an average,
3. Clover twice mown; two loads are grown;
4. Wheat; 22 bushels are reaped
5. Oats, or pease.

This is the course of Mr. CASSMAJOR, at North Mims. I objected to the fifth crop; but neither himself nor bailiff would admit any impropriety, on land well *dressed* with London compost.

But his course on wet land is:

1. Summer fallow;
2. Barley, four quarters are grown;
3. Clover, twice mown, and 2½ loads at the two, are grown;
4. Wheat; four to five loads are reaped;
5. Oats, pease, or beans; three to four quarters of either are the amount of the produce.

but the last crop, in either case, is only taken when land is in high order.

Here is a proof of the impropriety of the question, whether clover may safely be sown with barley on land in high order; the point, on which the objection to clover sown with barley on land summer-fallowed is founded.

I found a field of Mr. PRATCHET's, at Hatfield, farmed in a singular course for one round:

* A Hertfordshire load of wheat is equal to five bushels; a Yorkshire load to three; and a load in Hampshire, in its adjacent counties, and in the Midland Counties of England, is equal to forty.

1. Fallow,

1. Fallow,
2. Winter tares, come up the 18th of August,
3. Wheat,
4. Oats,

Mr. HALE, of King's Walden, and his steward, Mr. ROBERTS, also adopt the Norfolk course; but they sow no other grain after wheat.

Mr. LEACH follows the under-mentioned course:

1. Turnips,
2. Barley,
3. Clover,
4. Wheat,
5. Oats, or pease.

Then they return to turnips on some land; but on about 40 acres of gravel, he sows:

1. Turnips,
2. Barley,
3. Trefoil, white clover, ray-grass, common clover, fed,
4. Ditto, fed.
5. Ditto, fed.
6. Oats, on one earth.
7. Three earths are given immediately after oats, and then wheat is sown,
8. Winter fallow, for barley,
9. Grasses, as before, for three years;

and then the land is cultivated as above. Thus these 40 acres *neither want* nor have any manure, more than they receive from the feeding of the sheep on them, and from 60 bushels of ashes per acre, spread the first year on the grasses only, and 30 bushels of soot per acre on the wheat. It has answered greatly for 18 years to his full satisfaction.

He

He makes it a rule to feed his land as bare as possible, and always wishes not to let the ray run to bent.

Lady MELBOURNE has a field, which has been thus managed:

1. Potatoes were planted on it, and well manured, and the produce amounted to 400 bushels per acre;

2. Wheat was drilled on it, at the distance of nine inches. The crop amounted to seven loads, or 35 bushels, an acre;

3. Winter tares were next sown, for which 12l. an acre were this year offered; but they were mown for soiling; and at present the turnips after them are good;

4. Barley will be drilled next spring, as the fourth crop.

Mr. YOUNG, of Hurral, who farms on a large scale, with much intelligence, pursues the common course of taking oats or pease after wheat. It is extraordinary, to see how general this practice is; but if the clover is at all foul, he passes over this crop, and sows turnips.

The same course holds to St. Albans; and I found it steady on the fine farm of 483 acres of Mr. CLARKE, at Sandridgebury.

Mr. BIGGS, near that town, omits the oats after wheat, returning to fallow for turnips, instead of an after crop, except on 20 acres nearly in a year, which he sows with pease. Tares he sows on the wheat stubble, and grows good turnips the same year. On his heavier strong land, of which he has not much, his course of crops is:

1. Fallow,

2. Barley,

3. Pease,

4. Fallow,

4. Fallow,

5. Wheat,

6. Beans.

The common Hertfordshire course, of 1. Turnips, 2. Barley, 3. Clover, 4. Wheat, 5. Oats, continues about Watford, Rickmersworth, and all around Berkhamsted and Hempstead.

Mr. JENNENS, of the latter place, has a course,

1. Fallow,

2. Wheat,

3. Pease, drilled,

4. Barley,

5. Clover,

6. Wheat, but not in general, only as a variation from his common course.

Mr. COTTON, of the same place, observed, in defence of the common practice of taking oats after wheat, that they are the black oat, which, according to his opinion, succeeds best in land held together by roots, though of weeds, which will yield better than land in tilth, though clean ; and this makes a bad manager, in many cases, obtain a better crop of black oats than a good farmer would produce from the same land.

The old course continues to Beechwood and Market-Street ; where, if clover fails, they sow pease, followed either by turnips or summer fallow. They sow winter tares after wheat, three bushels per acre. They use them for feeding and soiling, and then fallow for turnips, or give a *bastard* * fallow for wheat; but the crop is not so good as on clover.

* Land not broken up until after Midsummer, to be sown with wheat in the following wheat season, is called a bastard fallow.

Round

Round Hitchin, in every direction, we find the old course of five shifts continued: it is varied by Mr. CHAP-MAN, of the Stamp-office, and a few others, by,

1. Turnips,
2. Barley,
3. Barley,
4. Clover,
5. Wheat;

and by some a sixth shift, of oats, is added.

In the open land they follow a course of,

1. Fallow,
2. Wheat, or barley,
3. Oats, or pease;

but sometimes sow turnips, by agreement, on the fallow.

The common turnip course continues about Welwyn, Wheathamsted, and Gorhambury.

Mr. SEDGWICK, of Rickmersworth, on stony land, pursues a course of,

1. Fallow,
2. Wheat,
3. Oats, or pease.

On dry land, this is the common course, but often turnips are sown after wheat. If a field grows so tired of clover as to want a change, their course is then:

1. Turnips,
2. Wheat,
3. Barley, or pease, or oats,
4. Turnips,
5. Barley,
6. Clover,
7. Wheat,
8. Oats.

Mr.

Mr. PARKER, at Munden, sows,

1. Turnips,
2. Barley,
3. Clover,
4. Wheat.

Upon this Mr. PARKER remarks, that by this course the land is favoured, as oats never follow wheat. If dung should run short, and a farmer not have it in his power to manure all his turnips, he may venture to sow a field of turnips without dunging, and succeed; a practice by no means to be depended on in the common rotation of taking oats after wheat. In order to favour the land, he has occasionally omitted sowing the clover, and taken pease for one round; but he suffered in his wheat; so that he scarcely knows what to do in the aukward circumstance of the failure of clover.

When clover fails at King's Langley, some farmers sow pease; others (but this is not common) fallow for wheat, and then take oats.

The Earl of ESSEX sows, near his farm-yard,

1. Tares, and then turnips,
2. Barley,
3. Clover,
4. Wheat;

and I saw at Cashiobury, very fine turnips after tares used in soiling, though sown twice and three times. This course affords much provender for the yard, in tares and clover for soiling, and turnips for stalls. In other parts of the farm, oats follow wheat.

At Cheshunt they sow,

1. Turnips,
2. Wheat,

3. Clover,

3. Clover,

4. Wheat;

also,

1. Fallow,

2. Wheat,

3. Oats, pease, or beans.

On the clays of Albury, Pelhams, &c. their course of crops is,

1. Fallow,	1. Fallow,
2. Wheat,	2. Barley,
3. Oats.	3. Pease.

Some courses consist of, 1. fallow; 2. wheat; 3. fallow; 4. barley; clover is also added with wheat, and oats and barley sometimes. They feed their clover in the spring; and then give a bastard fallow for wheat or barley.

In the extensive open fields about Barkway, we find,

1. Fallow,

2. Wheat,

3. Oats,

4. Fallow,

5. Barley,

6. Pease.

The same in the open fields (and all are open) about Royston. There are no enclosures in the parish, except small patches, quite in or near the town.

Mr. FOSTER, of Royston, practises a husbandry which long ago I publicly recommended; not that he took it from that recommendation, but his practice has confirmed it.

The Common Course.	*Mr. Foster's.*
1. Fallow,	1. Fallow,
2. Wheat,	2. Wheat,
	3. Oats,

3. Oats,	3. Clover and trefoil,
4. Fallow,	4. Ditto,
5. Wheat.	5. Wheat.

The seeds are sown on the wheat in March ; the first year he tops them in May, and then mows the ground for hay or seed. The second year the flock-master feeds them with the rest of the field ; but the grass entices the sheep to the spot, and dresses it consequently better than other parts ; and his following wheat has always been much superior to that fallowed ; even to the degree of beating that on which 3l. 4s. per acre have been bestowed in dressing ; a clear proof that so much fallowing is a real injury to the land. Besides this, he keeps two horses, in eight, fewer than before he practised this husbandry.

Mr. Doo, of Bygrave, is in the Norfolk four-shift course, leaving out the oats, taken so commonly in Hertfordshire. If clover fails, he sows turnips; and if turnips fail, carries on the fallow for barley. This is excellent husbandry.

Around Baldock, generally, but with some exceptions, oats are taken after the wheat.

Mr. SMITH, of Cloth-hall, has a course of,

1. Fallow,
2. Wheat,
3. Clover,
4. Oats, or barley ;

and the four-shift turnip course.

In the open field we find :

1. Turnips,
2. Barley,
3. Pease,
4. Fallow,

5. Wheat,

5. Wheat,

6. Oats: this by agreement.

In the open field near Baldock, we find another course by a singular agreement :

1. Turnips,

2. Barley,

3. Barley,

4. Clover ; which the parish flock-master eats till the last Thursday in May, then removes his sheep, and the farmer lets it stand for seed.

5. Wheat,

6. Oats.

REMARKS.

The first observation I have to make on the Hertfordshire courses, will be on the too general practice of taking a crop of oats after the clover-land wheat. This is extremely incorrect ; it is putting in a crop the fourth from the fallow ; for though clover is certainly to be esteemed a fallow respecting amelioration, yet, in that of cleaning land, it is by no means powerful : if there is any couch in land, it is sure to increase very considerably, while the land rests from tillage : this circumstance makes it such ill husbandry to leave broad clover a second year. To sow wheat on one ploughing, which can destroy no root-weeds, and then to put in a second crop of corn, must, in the nature of things, be injurious, by encouraging weeds. But what is the motive for this conduct ? Those who say that the land will bear it, simply assert that profit is thus to be gained, provided the land be kept in heart. I could never understand this, nor upon what principles the idea can be founded : and in order to place the question in the clearest light, it appears to me that nothing more can be necessary than

10

to contrast the two courses for any given number of years *.
Let us, for instance, compare them for 20 years, as in
that number both will begin with turnips, and both end
with corn †.

	Correct.					Incorrect.			
		£.	s.	d.			£.	s.	d.
1	Turnips,	2	0	0	1	Turnips,	2	0	0
2	Barley,	5	0	0	2	Barley,	5	0	0
3	Clover,	4	0	0	3	Clover,	4	0	0
4	Wheat,	7	0	0	4	Wheat,	7	0	0
5	Turnips,	2	0	0	5	Oats,	4	0	0
6	Barley,	5	0	0	6	Turnips,	2	0	0
7	Clover,	4	0	0	7	Barley,	5	0	0
8	Wheat,	7	0	0	8	Clover,	4	0	0
9	Turnips,	2	0	0	9	Wheat,	7	0	0
10	Barley,	5	0	0	10	Oats,	4	0	0
11	Clover,	4	0	0	11	Turnips,	2	0	0
12	Wheat,	7	0	0	12	Barley,	5	0	0
13	Turnips,	2	0	0	13	Clover,	4	0	0
14	Barley,	5	0	0	14	Wheat,	7	0	0
15	Clover,	4	0	0	15	Oats,	4	0	0
16	Wheat,	7	0	0	16	Turnips,	2	0	0
17	Turnips,	2	0	0	17	Barley,	5	0	0
18	Barley,	5	0	0	18	Clover,	4	0	0
19	Clover,	4	0	0	19	Wheat,	7	0	0
20	Wheat,	7	0	0	20	Oats,	4	0	0
		£. 90	0	0			£. 88	0	0

Hence

* In compliance with the opinion of the Member of the Board, to whom
these papers were referred, I had omitted the comparison; but a Hertfordshire
cultivator of eminence remonstrated so warmly against leaving it out, and
urged so strongly that he had, from my sketching such a table at his house,
converted a farmer to the opinion, that I could not but preserve it.—*A. Y.*

† The introduction of these calculations on imaginary data, are, with de-
ference

Hence it appears, that the correct course has a larger produce in 20 years than the incorrect one ; and this upon the supposition that the crops in both shall be equal throughout the whole period ; which is granting much more to bad farming than ought to be admitted. The crops in both cases are as follow :

Correct.	*Incorrect.*
5 Turnips,	4 Turnips,
5 Barley,	4 Barley,
5 Clover,	4 Clover,
5 Wheat.	4 Wheat,
	4 Oats.

Against four of oats, the good farmer has one of turnips, one of barley, one of clover, and one of wheat. In respect, therefore, of keeping live stock, the extra crops of turnips and clover, with the straw of the barley and wheat, will certainly exceed the straw of the four crops of oats. Manure, therefore, in one case, is greater than in the other.

And in point of cleaning the land, five crops of turnips, instead of four, will give here also a superiority to be added to that resulting from two crops of corn never coming together.

In whatever light, therefore, the comparison is viewed, it turns out decidedly in favour of the correct course.

Upon the courses in the clay district, in which the fallow system is found, I have one remark to offer : that they gain great crops in favourable years, is an undeniable fact ; but great as their expenses are, these exertions are little or no security against bad seasons, which form a very material

ference to the Author and the Hertfordshire cultivator, contrary to my decided opinion. It is allowed also at present, almost generally, that the four-shift course is the best; and hence, could they be correctly made, they would even then be unnecessary. I insert this note in justice to myself.—*H.*

deduc-

deduction from their profit. That husbandry, upon the long run, will be most beneficial, which is calculated by a variation of crops to be advantageous with a moderate produce: when a year's fallow and manuring are given to one crop, a moderate produce will not be a profitable return; if the farmer has not great success, he has loss; and consequently his hazard is considerable. The course I wish to see tried effectively is this:

1. Fallow, in partial compliance, not with mine, but with the opinion of others;
2. Barley,
3. Clover,
4. Beans,
5. Wheat.

All the manure should be laid for the beans. The fallow will secure barley. The clover will give good beans; and the beans, if well cultivated, are sure to give good wheat.

In answer to this I have been told, that beans will not do in this county; that they have been tried, &c. The trials made have been broad-cast, and therefore no rule whatever. They should be dibbled in double rows; that is, two furrows dibbled, a row on each, and then two or three furrows (according to soil and circumstances) should be missed, and two others dibbled, and so on; the intervals should also be well horse-hoed; the rows must be hand-hoed, and weeded, and the whole kept clean, like a garden. The soil is unquestionably well calculated for this crop; for similar land produces great beans in other counties, and therefore, if well managed, would do the same here. When beans are compared with fallow, let the consumption of the straw be considered, which yields excellent dung; let that dung be carried to the field which produces it, in

addi-

addition to the quantity the land receives in the present system ; a condition absolutely necessary, if the comparison be made fairly. Let these circumstances be duly attended to, and I have little doubt what the result will be.

But when random assertions are ventured, and the propriety of the recommendation questioned, I admit the fairness of all, if the proposal could be applied at once to a whole farm. But how very easy is it to try the experiment on three or four acres in perfect management, not merely for one season, good or bad, but to try such a quantity every year. It would then soon be ascertained, by a truly practical man, free from prejudices, whether the husbandry be really adapted to the land or not.

In the tillage preparatory to the beans, the Middlesex management should be adopted, of ploughing while the land is dry, *in autumn,* to throw the field into the destined form, it having been previously well gripped. Spring tillage should also be avoided, as it is pernicious on wet stiff soils, and nothing should require to be done then, except the planting of the field, when the weather would permit the work to proceed.

SECT. IV.—WHEAT.

THE information I received relative to the culture of this crop, may be properly arranged under the following heads :

1. Preparation,
2. Tillage,
3. Manuring,
4. Sort of wheat,
5. Quantity of seed,

6. Steep-

6. Steeping,
7. Time of sowing,
8. Treading,
9. Mildew,
10. Smut,
11. Cutting,
12. Produce,
13. Price,
14. Expenses,
15. Stubbles,
16. Threshing.

Preparation.—Mr. MARSH has had good experience in sowing wheat, both on clover lays and on fallow, and is decidedly of opinion, that the best and cleanest crops are after clover, as he finds his fallow wheat to be exceedingly inclined to weeds, even with his best management.

Mr. ROBERTS, bailiff to W. BAKER, Esq. at Bayfordbury, makes the same observation; the fallow wheat being very subject to the black bent.

Repeating the inquiry in many places, I found the opinion general through the county.

Tillage.—Mr. BYDE, in ploughing clover land for wheat, contrives to plough it some weeks before it is sown; which he, and all the best farmers, find much better than to harrow in the seed soon after the plough.

Mr. WHITTINGTON summer-fallowed a field of turnip land; and the turnips failing, he sowed it with winter tares: the crop was this year mown for hay, and as great as could grow; above two tons and a half per acre. He proposes to sow it this Michaelmas with wheat, *ploughed shallow.* I proposed to him merely to scuffle the surface, and not plough it, as I conceived that a year's fallow upon light land, and then so pulverizing a crop as tares, would

leave

leave the soil too loose, and hazard a root-falling crop. He admitted the reasoning, but observed, that very shallow ploughing would answer the same purpose, and leave a firm bottom for the wheat to root in.

In forming lands for wheat, the same gentleman substitutes for the common four-furrow ridge of three feet, lands of double the breadth, that admit of harrowing in the seed; which succeeds better than ploughing it in, as he finds, in the saving of seed; for in this way two bushels and one peck give as many plants as three bushels in the common way. This mode of reasoning may certainly be admissible, when applied to turnip lands; but it is questionable whether these flatter lands would do equally well on wetter soils. He justly remarks, that if the fallowing season has been unfavourable, they are obliged to stir the land while it is not in good order; and then, to make amends, they plough in the seed too deep for the crop, though not for the land; but the last earth may be to any right pitch, if the seed is to be harrowed in.

Mr. Young, of Hurral, in loose land subject in any degree to cause wheat to root-fall, takes care to plough the ley some time before the sowing, and he treads it well with stock.

When Mr. Hale's wheat shewed signs, in November and December, of being loose at the root, he drove his flock over, to tread down the land; and it did a great deal of good.

Mr. Sedgwick is clear, that it is highly beneficial to plough clover two, three, or four weeks before sowing, particularly if you plough early.

Manuring.—Under various heads descriptive of manuring in this county, I shall have occasion to mention the particular quantities applied for different crops. Here it is necessary only to mention, that in no district of the kingdom is wheat more generally top-dressed in the spring, with soot, ashes, and various other dressings; and I may add, that the farmers have a high opinion of this husbandry, and entertain no doubt of its answering well. But it deserves attention at the same time, that the small comparative quantity of natural grass which is found in the county, renders live-stock a very inferior object, and consequently the farm-yard dung much less than in counties abounding more in grass, and where hay and straw are in less demand for sale.

Sort.—I have rarely seen rivets, or bearded wheat, so common as at Sawbridgworth, on the clays and strong loams; on which soils it yields more amply than the red and white wheats; four or five quarters an acre, in a favourable year like the present (1801), are not uncommon.

They have a sort not uncommon, which I saw at Ware-Park, called polled rivets, which is very productive. Mr. BYDE has seen 100 grains in an ear.

Day's-stout, as it is called, is sown about St. Albans, and the ears generally grow with four sets of kernels. The same sort is sown also about Hitchin, where it was discovered originally by a poor man who first saw and collected an ear or two. Of this sort, Mr. CHAPMAN had last year none that yielded so well *.

At Rickmersworth, red Lammas and Burwell; so called from the place from whence it was brought, in Cambridgeshire; is a red wheat, and appears to be a red Lammas.

On the clays at Albury, &c. many rivets are sown, which have sometimes produced more than five quarters per acre; but this sort (as the growers of it say) is very

* I think the wheat called Day's-stout, by its description, must be what in ELLIS is called pirks, or pirky wheat.

uncer-

uncertain, and much subject to mildew: it sells badly, and the straw is worth but little. The farmers have them of the blue and white sort; the latter is preferred.

Seed. — In the clays and strong loams of Sawbridgworth, they sow two bushels of wheat per acre. On the same soil near Ware, three bushels on clover leys, and two and a half on fallows.

Mr. BYDE is very attentive to the change of seed: every third year he procures wheat from a distance; as from Burwell, in Cambridgeshire, and some from the Vale of Taunton: he changes this from his light to his heavy land once, and *vice versâ*; and the third year procures fresh seed from a distance. He changes also his barley from the Isle of Thanet, and also from Nottinghamshire. He has not the least doubt but that such attention and expense will answer well.

Mr. CLARKE, of Sandridgebury, sows three; about Berkhamsted, three are sown; at Hempstead, two and a half to three; at Beachwood the same.

A person at Hitchin sent his men into a field of wheat some years since, to plough it up; an old farmer going by, persuaded the men to go home: the wheat stood, and produced nine loads per acre. From three to three bushels and a half of seed were sown.

About the Grove, they sow from two bushels and a half to three bushels; at Rickmersworth, two and a half before Michaelmas, and three bushels after.

At Cheshunt two and a half are sown.

At Albury some sow two bushels, and others two and half a peck. It is here admitted, that the richest land requires the smallest quantity of seed of all sorts.

Two bushels and a half to three, according to soil and season, may be reckoned the general quantity sown, on an average per acre, throughout the county.

Steeps.

Steeps.—Mr. BYDE brines his wheat ; he swims it, but takes it out directly, and limes it. I found by his conversation, that he was not absolutely free from smut ; but being very careful in the purchase of seed, he does not find the inconvenience of this practice.

About Beachwood they make a brine with salt, which will swim a new-laid egg. They leave the seed from two to four hours in this brine, and stir and skim it : they lime it over night, and then sow it next morning ; but if it be kept a week, it will receive no injury. They are, however, not free from smut, and have much this year, and over the whole country, even from Watford. At Hempstead market some wheat sold for 55s. per load, and some for 31s. 6d. ; the difference was occasioned by the smut.

This malady might be easily prevented ; and remedies for it are printed in the Annals of Agriculture.

A steeping of one hour is trusted to at King's Walden. If chamber-ley be added, or thrown on the seed after brining, it kills the wheat.

Mr. LEACH has bought smutty wheat, to sow for curiosity, and even the worst which he could find : he steeped it six hours in a very strong brine, made to swim a large egg : he dried it with hot lime, and sowed it directly, and had no smut. He has tried this several times, always with success. He steeps clean wheat but three hours.

Mr. SEDGWICK steeps his seed in brine, as above, six hours ; then dries it with lime, and sows it directly ; and he never has any smut : he omitted it three or four years, and suffered severely by such omission.

Time of Sowing.—Mr. STEPHENSON, manager for the Marchioness of SALISBURY, observes, in relation to the culture of all crops at Hatfield, that early sowing is perhaps

haps a circumstance as important as any other that can be named. Certain favourable seasons will sometimes agree with late sowings, but upon an average of years, the early ones are almost sure to be the best. Mr. CASSMAJOR, of North Mims, and his experienced bailiff, ROBERTS, unite in this opinion.

Mr. ROBERTS, of King's Walden, has been for some years in the habit of sowing common wheat in the spring, after turnips, and has thus had very great success. In the harvest of 1800 he had ten acres, which produced five loads per acre; and all the rest of his wheat did not produce three. He has a great opinion of this practice on any soil here, whether light or heavy; but it should not be ventured after the middle of February. They sow two bushels and three pecks per acre.

Mr. LEACH reckons, that, in general, the best season is from the middle of September to the middle of October *.

Mr. SEDGWICK considers a fortnight before and a fortnight after Michaelmas, as the best time; but at all events in a wet season.

Treading.—Mr. YOUNG, of Hurral, top-folds his wheat after it is up, with much success, even on land that does not particularly demand treading. Mr. BIGGS, near St. Albans, top-folds after sowing, but desists just at the moment of its coming up; and thinks this practice on dry loam very advantageous.

Mr. SEDGWICK, on light lands, always folds after sowing, and till Christmas, and finds great benefit from it. After very wet nights, and the ground has been poached, he has scolded his shepherd, but the wheat has been the better. When he observes a piece of wheat failing, from red worm or grub, &c. he spreads turnips

* I am most decidedly of his opinion.—*H.*

on

on it, and brings the flock to eat them, and tread the land;
and it has always answered well. This certainly is a
very valuable hint, much deserving attention *.

Mildew.—Mr. WHITTINGTON always cuts mildewed
wheat as early as possible; for it improves nothing by
standing †.

Smut.—There seems to be no security against this dis-
temper in any part of the county; yet under the article
Steeps, it is seen that they generally pickle the seed. This
disorder must, therefore, arise from the too general practice of only wetting the seed with the brine, or of steeping it too short a time; and very possibly from swim-
ming too much together, by which the skimming of it is
very much impeded †.

Cutting.— Straw in this county being very valuable,
from the vicinity of London, the farmers are generally
attentive to cut pretty close, but not nearly so much so as
in some parts of Surrey. I found that Mr. WHITTING-
TON did not neglect this point, for he has both *bagged* his
wheat almost close to the ground, and some he has mown
with a scythe and a cradle. A trussed load sells at home
for 40s.

There is much about Hatfield mown with a scythe and
cradle, and then bound. Rewards are given for mowing
and binding, per acre; but it is reckoned a slovenly prac-

* I had a field of wheat sown on a bad clover ley, which clover had been
sown with barley. The barley, to the extent of more than an acre and a half,
had been eat by the grub, in my absence, and the red clover was indifferent. The wheat had scarcely appeared, when we had every reason to apprehend its destruction by the grub. I ordered some lime to be taken from
an adjoining building, where it lay for the masons' use, and spread over it
immediately, and the wheat to be rolled by a double horse-roller. The bailiff objected to it, as the horses' feet would destroy the wheat, the season
being rather inclined to wet : I persisted, however, and destroyed the grub;
and the wheat in this part was good at harvest, and as good as any of the
field.—*H*.

† These opinions are just.—*H*.

tice,

tice, beating out much of the corn ; and, by the farmers cutting it too low, many weeds are carried into the barn.

Some wheat is bagged at Rickmersworth.

Produce.—At Sawbridgworth, Mr. PARRIS gets seven or eight loads this year on fallow, and nearly as much on clover and pease; but this average, *communibus annis,* amounts only to 5 loads, or 25 bushels.

At Ware, Mr. BYDE expects nine loads per acre in some fields. The turnip soils produce, on an average, from 17 to 20 bushels, and strong land returns about 25 bushels.

At Hadham, on their strong land, the average is from 25 to 26 bushels.

On the fine rich loams of Buntingford, 40 bushels are by no means an uncommon crop.

Mr. GREG's bailiff shewed me some very fine crops: they never had a better crop in this county than the present.

Mr. WHITTINGTON estimates the produce of all farms, on an average, at 23 bushels per acre.

The Rev. Mr. KEATE, at Hatfield, on a good 20s. loam, but on a bottom that wants hollow-draining, and with very excellent management in manuring, gets generally 6 loads an acre, 30 bushels: sometimes $6\frac{1}{2}$, and even 7.

Mr. STEPHENSON, by calculating 12 sheaves to yield a bushel, estimates Lady SALISBURY's wheat this year at 9 loads 3 bushels per acre.

About Sandridge and St. Albans, the average amounts to 24 bushels.

The produce about Berkhamsted runs from 4 to 6 loads; at Hempstead, to 4 loads; about Beachwood, to $4\frac{1}{2}$; and at Hitchin, to 5.

The wheat-fields about King's Walden return 4 bushels;

and

and those of Mr. HALE, this year, 7, or more; and I can easily believe it, from the appearance of his stubbles; equally stout and clean. They do credit to his husbandry. At Horlwell they grow as much.

Around Gorhambury, 25 bushels are the average: this year Lord GRIMSTON has 30.

About the Grove, 4 loads are grown. The fields of Mr. LEACH produce 5 loads per acre about four times in 18 years.

The fields at Rickmersworth give 4 loads; and those at Cheshunt 6 to 7 loads; and this is not very uncommon.

Twenty-four Bushels are grown at Albury, through the parish. Mr. CALVERT has had five quarters an acre round, on a large farm, as he himself informed me.

Around Barkway, three loads and a half are produced.

Mr. HILL, of Whittle, informs me that he has had 119 loads 4 bushels, from 12 acres 1 rood—a small fraction less than 50 bushels per acre. It was on a clover ley, mown twice for hay, having been ashed at the rate of 80 bushels per acre, and the wheat had 45 bushels of soot per acre.

They grow about Royston, three to three loads and a half without, and four and a half or five, with manure.

The produce around Baldock amounts to four loads, or near that quantity; but Ashwell, a poor open parish, grows not more than three.

At Cloth-hall, four loads are grown.

Crop of 1800.—Mr. BYDE being applied to for his opinion of this crop, made an experiment which convinced him of the reality of the scarcity, and he made it by threshing

clover-

clover-wheat grown on land of 12s. per acre, and fallow-wheat produced on land of 20s. He threshed nine quarters, three bushels of each. Of the clover-wheat, four London marketable loads of straw yielded that quantity; of the fallow-wheat, 9 loads. A bushel of the clover-wheat weighed 67 lb.; of the fallow-wheat, 57. Seventeen pecks of flour were produced from 5 bushels of clover-wheat; and from 5 bushels of the fallow, 15. Thus the deficiency of the crop, both in quantity and quality, from the best land, was ascertained; and consequently the probability of a general deficiency.

Mr. CLARKE, of Sandridgbury, procured an account of 32 parishes; the average produce 12½ bushels per acre, as he informed me.

Price.—" With an average crop, what ought to be the price of wheat?" This was a question which I asked of many intelligent farmers. The general answer was, not less than 7s. 6d. per bushel. In January 1780, Mr. WHITTINGTON sold the best wheat at 22s. 6d. per load, and bad at 15s.; in January 1797, at 34s. 6d. the load; in January 1798, at 30s. 6d.; in January 1800, at 60s.

Mr. ROOK conceives, that if 20 farmers are taken, occupiers indiscriminately of all sized farms, small as well as great, that the average result of the high price of corn will not be found beneficial; that the little ones will have lost as much as some of the great ones have gained.

The present crop (1801) exceeds an average one by four bushels an acre. The price ought to be 40s. per load.

At Barkway I had the good luck to meet a company of very intelligent farmers and commissioners, who agreed, that if wheat should be, for the next seven years, lower than

than from 9s. to 10s. a bushel, the farmer would not have a price proportioned to his increased expenses.

At Royston, they said that wheat should be 10s. ; barley 5s. ; and oats 2s. 6d.

Twenty shillings per acre, has been paid at Cheshunt for ploughing.

It is unnecessary to enter here into calculations in confirmation of what those farmers and commissioners advanced : a moment's reflection on the greatly increased expenses of the farmer, compared with the amount of those expenses in former years ; and on the then price of corn, compared also with that for which it now sells, will decidedly clear up the point, and prove that the price, as stated by them, is not so high, in proportion to the farmers' present expenses, now, as the prices, twenty years since, were to the farmers' expenses of that time.

At the time of my revising these notes (October 1801), wheat in the markets of this neighbourhood (Suffolk) is from 27s. to 30s. a comb, of four bushels, or 54s. to 60s. a quarter. It is therefore a good deal below what the Hertfordshire farmers think a price *necessary*, when compared with the expenses at which they carry on their business. It is true, that poor-rates will fall considerably with the price of corn, but not proportionably : rents are much raised, and are not likely to fall ; tithes are the same : labour also has advanced, and is not likely, nor ought it to be reduced. Hence it becomes a vast object with the legislature of the kingdom, to take such measures as to prevent a too great depression of price. They are not at all likely to do this with a view to the benefit of the farmers ; but they ought to do it as preventing a scarcity, and very high prices. Nothing but a steady

security

security against too low a price for wheat, can prove a
real security against its being too high. And it ought never to be out of the minds of those whose ideas may have
influence in Parliament, that the low price, from 1771 to
1794 (5s. 8d. a bushel, on the average of the kingdom),
has had a material effect in causing the late melancholy
scarcities. Many years since, 6s. a bushel was a reasonable
price; and a much better one for the farmers than 8s. at
present. While the corn laws are suffered to remain under those modern changes in system which have almost
proved the ruin of the kingdom, there can be no hope of
preventing very great and mischievous alternations in
price—ever either too low or too high. This is a subject
upon which it would be easy to expatiate: I have treated
it amply for above thirty years *, pointing out so long
ago the errors of the new system: time has sanctioned
the opinion; and it is earnestly to be hoped that the result
of so long experience will not be lost, when these laws
shall receive that revision which is become essentially necessary to the welfare of the kingdom.

Stubbles.—I know no district in which they are so attentive to cutting stubble as in Herts, carting it carefully
to the farm-yards to make manure.

Some few persons are of a different opinion, and think
it better to plough them in, as in Norfolk: but when
the quantity of yard-dung is considered, which is made
merely by this practice, where cattle, or sheep, or hogs,
are kept in sufficient numbers properly to effect it, I have
no doubt of the Hertfordshire practice being far superior.

Threshing.—It is every where a very general custom
to thresh by the day; and I am informed that they throw

---

* Expediency of a Free Exportation of Corn, 8vo. 1769. Second edition,
1770. Political Arithmetic, 8vo. 1774.

the

the grain out of the chaff every night, and take a day to dress 10 loads (50 bushels). I learn also, that they estimate five loads as a common day's work, unless the crop shall be indifferent. The mode of threshing the straw for the London market, with a perpendicular stroke, rather than a loose slanting one, as in other counties, certainly facilitates the labourer's work; and the farmer finds his loss in corn, compensated by the extraordinary high price for which he sells his straw.

SECT. V.—BARLEY.

THE intelligence received concerning this crop, demands only the following heads, as to,

1. Ploughing for a crop,
2. The sort,
3. The seed,
4. The produce.

Ploughing.—Mr. BYDE ploughs his turnip land thrice, if eaten off in time for such tillage; but if late, he gives it only one earth.

I have found it the general practice through a considerable district, to plough the turnip land but once: very few ever give it more tillage.

Mr. YOUNG, of Hurral, remarks, that it is of great consequence to give the ploughing for barley in a dry season, when the land will work well; in which case, clover may safely be sown at the time of sowing barley; it will not be of too quick a growth for the corn: but if the soil shall be in too moist a state, then the barley will be checked, and the clover will get a-head.

In

In several trials in breaking up new heath land, barley failed. Oats are the proper crop for some years.

Mr. CHAPMAN, of Hitchin, ploughs twice for barley, after turnips.

Lord GRIMSTON finds that *combing** the turnip land before the seed earth, is beneficial.

The general practice, to which exceptions a) very few, is to plough turnip land but once for this grain. Now it is remarkable, that in Norfolk, upon a much looser and more friable soil, even on sand itself, they give three earths; and the same practice is pursued in Suffolk, and many other well cultivated districts. The argument against it in Hertfordshire is, the want of time, after turnips are eaten off; but this can no more be admitted in one county than in another, unless it may arise from some local circumstance, which wants explanation. I am inclined to attribute it to the sale of hay and straw at London: this occasions much regular work, attended with as regular a receipt of cash, and probably causes this insufficient tillage: to save two earths at a busy season, is a flattering circumstance; and this tempts them perhaps to act contrary to their judgment. It is not necessary to adopt an universal rule: on soils that are liable to close and run together in spring tillage, when the turnip land breaks up in very friable order, were it not sown at once, and were rains to succeed, much time might be lost before two more earths could be given while the land would be in due temper, that is, dry enough, to receive them. Such cases may demand sowing on one earth; but on drier soils, where rain is not equally to be feared, it cannot be good husbandry to sow on one earth two seeds (barley and clover), for both of which the land cannot be, in the far-

* A mode of half ploughing.

mer's

mer's language, too fine and *full of tilth*. It becomes
therefore an inquiry, with respect to this management, as
well as to many others on a Hertfordshire farm, how far
from London it really answers to carry hay and straw thi-
ther; where they can go twice a week only, thrice, or
once every day. This is not the place to discuss the question, but it was necessary incidentally to mention it.

Sort.—Zealand winter barley has been sown at Albury,
and produced nine or ten quarters an acre; but the grain
so bad, as to be good for nothing but pigs and poultry. It
is sown in autumn, and harvested much earlier than the
common sort.

Seed.—The usual quantity, of four bushels, is sown
every where in the county; but Mr. BYDE has tried of
late a smaller quantity, proportioned to the richness of the
soil and preparation. This year he sowed only two, and
two and a half, and thinks his crop as good as if he had
sowed more.

Four bushels, about Hitchin, is the usual quantity; but
Mr. CHAPMAN has gone as far as five.

Three bushels are sown about the Grove; and about
Rickmersworth, three and a half, and sometimes four bushels, may be set down as the general average quantity
throughout this county.

Produce.—In Mr. BYDE's considerable experience, he
never but once met with an ear of barley containing 40
grains. This year he has plucked several of 38, in his
crops.

The strong land at the Hadhams, yields, on an average,
on fallow, 36 bushels.

On the strong lands at Westmill, near Buntingford,
five quarters are grown.

Mr. WHITTINGTON estimates the general average
produce at 32 bushels per acre.

The

The general average about St. Albans, and Sandridge, amounts to four quarters.

Mr. BIGGS, when he lived at Stanstead, in this county, had once 10 quarters per acre.

About Berkhamsted, they plough the turnip land once; sow four bushels; the medium crop amounts to four quarters; from three and a half to six. The same crops are found at Hempstead and Beachwood.

About Hitchin, the average produce, as Mr. CHAPMAN thinks, does not exceed three quarters and a half; which appears to me to be a low estimate for the soil.

About King's Walden, four quarters are produced; about Gorhambury, five; and a good crop gives six.

We find about the Grove, three quarters and a half; at Rickmersworth, scarcely four quarters.

At Albury, five quarters are grown after a fallow; but the crop after turnips is much less.

Around Barkway, three quarters and a half are produced

About Royston, three to four quarters are grown; but barley is an uncertain crop on chalk.

Around Baldock we find four quarters, with good management; but more generally three: and barley is very uncertain on chalk; for if sown late in spring, it fails, if the season be not very favourable indeed.

Cloth-hall grows four quarters.

The average crop, extracted from seventeen minutes made of crops, gives 32 bushels and a small fraction.

SECT. VI.—OATS.

UNDER this article, the information concerns only,

1. The tillage,
2. The seed,
3. The cutting,
4. The produce.

Tillage.—Mr. PICKFORD, in breaking up a heath, of a soil rather loose, ploughed once for black oats; and, to consolidate the soil in wet weather, harrowed them in, and then picked up 50 loads of furz roots on 50 acres, which causing much trampling and carting, in the same wet season answered, and gave a very good crop.

Seed.—The common quantity amounts to five bushels per acre. Mr. BYDE sows four.

All from Hatfield to St. Albans, Watford, Berkhamsted, &c. sow four bushels; but about Hitchin, from four to five.

About the Grove, they sow three bushels of black and four of white.

To multiply minutes would be useless; for the general practice through the county is to sow four bushels.

Cutting.—They are commonly mown either with the naked scythe, or a cradle added, and carted loose; but the Earl of CLARENDON has tried binding them after mowing, and with such success, that his Lordship purposes continuing the practice.

Produce.—Mr. WHITTINGTON estimates the average produce at 32 bushels per acre.

About

About Berkhamsted, four quarters and a half are produced: this year six or seven.

At Beachwood, &c. four quarters and a half are grown, and about Hitchin, four quarters.

About King's Walden, we find the same quantity. Mr. HALE had this year eight, after Swedish turnips: I have seldom seen finer stubbles than those which I found on his farm.

About Gorhambury, five quarters are grown.

The Grove gives four quarters.

About Rickmersworth, four and a half are produced; and about Albury, three and a half; but around Barkway, only three quarters; while Royston gives three to three and a half; and Cloth-hall three and a half.

We find four quarters to be the general average.

SECT. VII.—PEASE.

MR. WHITTINGTON sows the large maple pea, under furrow, between old and new Christmas, as the best time; the Marlboroughs much later.

Mr. PICKFORD, at Market-street, sows the *hedge* pea with great success on new land: the crops are large, and uncommonly podded.

Mr. LEACH has found pease a very hazardous crop; but, for these two years past, has ploughed in the seed in the beginning of February; and, when the plants have been four inches high, he has harrowed the ground in a dry season twice, across and across, and rolled it immediately. His crops are good, and of the Berkshire dun.

Mr. NEWMAN HATLEY, at King's Langley, drills pease, by sowing them in *combs* (see *Ploughing*), and hand-hoes them clean: he finds the crops much better than when they are broad-cast.

HERTS.]   Mr.

Mr. SEDGWICK, of Rickmersworth, prefers the Marlborough grey : four bushels and a half produce a good crop, equal to four quarters. Mr. SEDGWICK drills his corn in rows, nine inches asunder, with a small drill.

Mr. FOSTER, at Royston, when he began farming, and for some years, was very free in sowing pease, and often on the same land; but he soon saw his error; and found that, when this plant is repeated on the land without an interval of many years, they fail and blight; an unlucky circumstance, as pease are so much more favourable to land than oats.

About Dunstable, " they never sow the same land with " pease but once in nine years, and consider an interval " of eleven years better*."

SECT. VIII.—BEANS.

I SAW very few beans in the eastern part of the county, and the few which I did see, were ill managed; the first information that I had worth noting, was from Mr. YOUNG, at Hurral, in Hatfield, who dibbles them in the Middlesex way, across the lands, in rows 16 inches asunder, two bushels on an acre, hand-hoeing them twice, earthing them up the second time : he sows wheat after these with success.

Mr. BIGGS, near St. Albans, dibbles them in rows across the lands, four or five pecks on an acre. He pays 9d. a peck for labour, and hand-hoes them twice : he esteems 30 bushels to be a fair crop, but has had 60, which is a vast crop.

Mr. COTTON, of Hempstead, drills his rows at the distance of 22 inches ; horse-hoes them well. The common,

* First Report.

flinty,

flinty, strong land of the country, so cultivated, produces fine crops.

Mr. BATTEN, of Welwyn, compared two acres of broad-cast beans with two drilled in rows, distant 18 inches ; both crops were well hand-hoed : the drilled produced double the quantity reaped on the broad-cast.

In the parishes of Watford, Rickmersworth, and Bushy, we find three or four hundred acres of clay land without flints, on which the bean husbandry is practised in the course of fallow, wheat, beans ; the last are dibbled in across the lands by women, who do it by lines : the field is kept clean by hand-hoeing, and produces, on an average of seven years, four quarters per acre. Some sow horse-beans, some ticks : they plough after Christmas for them, and set them in February, or in the beginning of March.

Between Elstree and Barnet also, the same husbandry is found.

At Cheshunt, &c. many beans are sown broad-cast ; but they are drilled at the distance of 18 inches by Mr. RUSSEL, and hand-hoed thrice : wheat follows. That gentleman shewed me some bean-stalks, on one of which I counted 58 pods. He also drills pease. Mr. SAUNDERS, his neighbour, has adopted the same husbandry.

The culture of beans might form a very interesting branch in the husbandry of Hertfordshire, but they are too much neglected ; nor do the farmers understand the great importance of making these a preparation for wheat. Fallows upon their strong lands, can be lessened advantageously upon a large scale only, by means of the bean culture. The practice of that great and excellent farmer, Mr. YOUNG, of Hurral, should excite attention to this profitable husbandry*.

SECT.

* Much has been said on fallows ; but unless beans shall be well drilled, and turnips also, the one on heavy, the other on light land, and shall be not only
hoed

SECT. IX.——BUCK-WHEAT.

VERY litle of this plant is found in the county.

Mr. LEACH sows about the middle of May, one bushel per acre ; on good land, three pecks. The crop ripens, and is mown, in the beginning of September: it produces from two to seven loads. It is very good food for horses with bran, and is ground for store-pigs with pollard ; but too hot alone. It is most excellent for pigeons. It fouls the land by scattering its seed, which comes up in the spring in the next crop*.

SECT. X.——POTATOES.

MORE are planted in Sawbridgeworth and its vicinity this year than for many years past. Mr. PLUMMER, at Gilston, has a very luxuriant crop, in double rows, on six-feet ridges. Whole fields are set about Harlow, where Mr. MONTAGU BURGOYNE informs me, that he sold at a reasonable price to the amount of 500l. last year.

Mr. BYDE gives a hedge-rein to several of his men, on which they plant potatoes. The land being old grass and rich, I found their crops very fine and luxuriant.

About Stevenage very few are cultivated, and even many cottagers that have gardens, neglect this important object.

hoed once, twice, or thrice, but also kept continually clean by repeated hand and horse-hoeings, the system of no fallows can never be pursued without evident disadvantage, and even ruin, to the farmer who may practise it. Much injury has been done by the injudicious manner in which the system of no fallows has been recommended.—*H.*

* This crop should be harvested when the seed is nearly ripe : when suffered to be dead ripe, great loss ensues.—*H.*

Mr.

Mr. Penrose, of Hatfield, has often sown wheat after potatoes, but very rarely gets a good crop; finding this culture, as I was informed, a bad preparation for that grain.

Mr. Cassmajor, at North Mims, has cultivated this root, and has had considerable crops, but he uniformly found it so exhausting, that he could never get such crops of corn after them as satisfied him; he therefore gave up the culture.

Mr. Marsh, near Hatfield, a very improving farmer, has cultivated this root for some years: he manures with horse-dung; plants chiefly the champion sort, and gets 500 to 600 bushels per acre. He has had good wheat after them, but better crops of barley.

Mr. Newman, of Bayford, has fed cattle on potatoes, but as they were too watry, they would not answer; he therefore left off the practice.

Mr. Rooper, of Berkhamsted, has usually had four or five acres for fifteen years past; he thinks very differently from Mr. Newman, and uses them raw for fatting beasts, as he assures me, with much success; for hogs also they answer very well. He plants them after oats in every third furrow; and ridges up the stubble soon after harvest: he harrows it down in the spring, and spreads eight loads of long fresh dung per acre; then plants near 20 bushels per acre: he horse-hoes and ploughs up the crop, which produces from 150 to 200 bushels per acre, on a flinty loam, or a chalk bottom. Wheat will not do after them; but the barley is good. They are, he is clear, a very exhausting crop.

Mr. Hale, of King's Walden, has generally a small field, of an acre or two, and sows oats after them, the crops of which are very good.

Mr. Hill, of Whittle, is a great cultivator of this root. I called, but he was absent; meeting him, however,

after-

afterwards at Barkway, he informed me that he has generally four acres: that he has had 1100 bushels on two acres
and a half. He finds that the giving them to store hogs
is the most profitable application. His men dig up the
crop with four-pronged forks, at 1d. per bushel; which
crop is easily measured by a fifteen-bushel cart.

Mr. KING, of Barkway, has this year 36 acres in the
open field, put in without manure.

N. B. The field is under an act of enclosure.

He has had wheat after potatoes, but not good crops:
this year he will take barley, which he is well convinced
is the most profitable management.

" Mr. HILL has a field of uniformly light sand loam,
" on the ridge or highest land in the parish of Kempton,
" containing about two acres and three-quarters; this
" field was cropped with potatoes in 1794, when I saw
" it, and the year before produced about 400 bushels per
" acre, worth on the average 1s. 9d. per bushel—35l.
" per acre: every attendant expense about 5l.—30l. clear.
" He fed his milch cows and store-pigs with the potatoes
" in winter: the cows gave abundance of milk, but not
" cream in proportion*."

SECT. XI.—TURNIPS.

THIS most useful plant was cultivated very early in
Hertfordshire, as a general article of husbandry; and I
believe, before they were commonly introduced in Norfolk: it is natural, therefore, to expect to find them in
great perfection: this, however, is not the case in one
very material point.

* First Report.

A cir-

A circumstance in the culture of this crop, which Mr.
BYDE has found of very great consequence, is that of
ploughing in the seed, instead of harrowing it in on the
surface : he has found in this management, that it is not
nearly so liable to be destroyed by the fly. He ploughed it
in on half a field, and harrowed it in on the other half ; and
the difference was so considerable, as to convince his bailiff,
whose opinion was adverse to the practice. When the season proves too dry, it makes the difference of crop or no
crop. He ploughs in the Swedish turnip also, and with
equal success.

Mr. BYDE has received 1s. per week per head, for his
turnips, sold by him to be fed on the land with sheep.

From Hertford to Hatfield I found the turnips over-run
with charlock in full blossom ; and round Hatfield, the
same ; on inquiry, I learned that they hoe them but once :
this is a declension instead of improvement in Hertfordshire
husbandry.

Mr. YOUNG, of Hurral, often hoes twice, but not always. Mr. BAKER's bailiff, ROBERTS, does the same.
The former always manures well for this crop. He prefers,
first, yard-dung from beasts fed on oil-cake ; then hog-
dung, and then the sheep-fold.

About St. Albans they seldom hoe more than once.

Mr. BIGGS, of Bursten, near St. Albans, has ploughed
in turnip-seed shallow, and found it sometimes advantageous.

About Berkhamsted they plough four times, and always manure either with dung or ashes ; they hoe in general but once ; some sow twice, and feed all with sheep.

Mr. JENNENS, of Hempstead, sowed turnips broad-
cast where he had intended to have drilled them, but had
been prevented ; he horse-hoed them, however, into rows,
and

and they did so well as to exceed most in their vicinity. He manured his land previously with malt-dust.

About Beachwood, &c. they plough four times, sow three pounds of seed, hoe once, at 6s. or 7s. per acre ; all are eaten by sheep: the price paid for them, when sold, was from 2l. to 3l. All manure for turnips in preference to wheat, and with farm-yard dung, or with the fold.' Sir JOHN SEBRIGHT has tried the Norfolk way of dunging for wheat, by spreading it first for turnips. The country will not be much indebted to him for this plan : their own is much better.

Around Hitchin they give four or five earths ; sow two pounds ; no more on chalk than on gravel ; some few hoe twice ; all are fed on the land by sheep.

Lord GRIMSTON, at Gorhambury, and a few others, hoe twice, and many but once : all are fed with sheep, except a few which are drawn. They sell from 40s. to 4l. to be eat on the land.

Mr. SEDGWICK, of Rickmersworth, hoes twice, but in common only once ; he prefers the long stable-dung, as manure for the turnip culture.

From these notes it appears, that the general practice is to hoe but once ; which is a most reprehensible fault in their husbandry : every motive should incline them to the necessary exertion of giving a second hoeing. In Norfolk, Suffolk, and other counties, if weeds appear, the good farmers will look their crops over a third time : here they are contented with fields yellow with charlock. I hope, that to name such bad management is sufficient : every one must admit that it is a point deserving a better attention.

Mr. MARSH, near Hatfield, has a crop of what I have seen under the name of Jerusalem sprouts ; a sort of kale, the whole produce of which is leaf, and which bears feeding

ing repeatedly: it has been recommended to him as of great value for sheep: this is the first year since it has been cultivated by him.

SECT. XII.—SWEDISH TURNIPS.

THIS is an article of culture which gives me much pleasure to register, for it manifests an uncommon degree of merit. In other parts of the kingdom, these turnips are met with in the farms of gentlemen, but rarely in those of tenants; but in Hertfordshire, they have so rapidly made their way, as to be found in the usual management of great numbers of the common farmers: no trivial proof of their observation, knowledge, and good sense.

Mr. BYDE has this year 25 acres of them; a very regular plant, promising a great produce. He finds that sheep will not touch the common turnip, if they can get at these; but they are apt to break their teeth, from the greater hardness and solidity of the root. He finds that they do not taint the milk of cows, like the common turnip; and are an useful food for horses. He sows them from the 13th of May to the 20th of June. When sown very early, as in May, they are so difficult to keep clean, that he prefers June. Mr. BYDE reaps better crops of barley after them than after common turnips.

From Ware to Hadham, and thence to Standon, I believe I saw eight or ten fields of this plant, and most of them very fine and vigorous.

Mr. GREG, at Westmill, has 25 acres; he has cultivated this crop for some years, and generally on a large scale. He manures for them with yard-muck, or pulverized rape-cake, from 6 to 20 bushels an acre, according

to

to the soil, usually with about 12; and sows the seed early in May. He states them, from his experience, to be much better than common turnips; as they never rot, let the weather be as severe as it may, nor are they stringy, when consumed late in the spring. He informs me that the barley after them is not so good as after other turnips eat earlier, but much better when those turnips are consumed as late as the Swedish; that they do not cost more in cultivation, yet are of double the value. The farmers sow them very generally, so that few are to be found who sow none.

Mr. WHITTINGTON, at Broadwater, is a considerable cultivator of this plant. He prefers them to common turnips, and could he have more time for preparation, would substitute them for the greatest part of that crop. He sows soon after the first week in May: for value in feeding, time of consumption, duration, &c. he knows nothing equally valuable.

The Rev. Mr. KEATE, at Hatfield, is also considerable in this cultivation, and with much success: he has had crops of them for five years. His crop this year amounts to five acres, which I viewed with great pleasure—a fine regular plant, very luxuriant, equally set out, and quite clean. They were well manured with yard-dung, and the land ploughed four times. He sows in the middle of June: they had been hoed at the expense of 7s. per acre: part of the field had yielded a crop of winter tares. They have usually come to a large size on Mr. KEATE's farm. He has fed horses with them, entirely to his satisfaction; and cuts the roots with a very simple, effective turnip-slicer: each horse had a bushel every day, with chaff, but no oats; they did their work very well, but in spring-sowing had a few oats added: they throve well, and became fat while they were eating this turnip. Cows also do well on it; nor does

does it give their milk or butter any taste, but increases their milk considerably. They are excellent also for fattening sheep. The culture is become very general through the country; so that there are few farmers in it who are without a field of this excellent plant.

The Marchioness of SALISBURY has many acres in great perfection, and finds them of incomparable use. But Mr. STEPHENSON remarks, that their most important use is so late in the spring, that it is difficult to introduce them in a regular course, and sow spring corn in time: he thinks them rather applicable to a few fields out of a regular rotation for sowing some other crop than barley or oats after them; such, for instance, as winter tares. I may add, buck-wheat also. Cows do very well on Swedish turnips without hay, and give much milk; and these roots last longer for sheep in consumption than an equal quantity of common turnips, but the sheep do not thrive equally.

Mr. PRATCHET, of Hatfield, always has some Swedish turnips for the latter part of the season, and approves of them greatly.

Mr. DEERMAN, of Astwick, is a great friend to them; but observes, that they throw the land out of course; as they are most useful so late in the season, that spring corn cannot be sown after them, he thinks the best way is to sow common turnips for the next crop, by which means also the land would be brought into remarkably high order. Mr. MARSH, his neighbour, makes the same observation, but has, however, always sown spring-corn after them.

Mr. CLARKE, of Sandridgbury, has cultivated them eight or nine years with great success; generally 20 to 25 acres. He sows the last week in May, and finds no difficulty with the succeeding crop, which is always barley,

and

and as good as any, and often the best on his farm. He has eat them so late as the 6th of May *.

Mr. BIGGS, near St. Albans, has sown them these six years; generally, the last week in May, or the first in June, and sows barley for his next crop; but if they are consumed very late, he sows white oats.

Mr. WANGFORD, at Bushy, sows none; and there are very few in this part of the county: they are not here in estimation.

About Berkhamsted they are just introduced.

Mr. COTTON, at Hempstead, cultivates, and has the highest opinion of them; and has only one objection to them—their slow growth, which retards their hoeing. His corn grown after them is good.

Sir JOHN SEBRIGHT cultivates them, and has a very high opinion of their merit.

Mr. PICKFORD, at Market-street, has 30 acres this year, a beautifully regular crop (see *Waste Lands*). He has from experience a great opinion of them, when applied to the fatting of oxen and sheep, and to the feeding of hogs; in which last application he thinks them superior to potatoes. I saw above 500 hogs on his farm. On finding these roots so profitable, he grew no more potatoes.

Mr. CHAPMAN, of Hitchin, is of opinion that this root demands a richer and stronger soil than the chalks and loams about Hitchin; for they have been cultivated some years, dunged for, and twice hoed, but the success has not been great. The farmers entertain a high opinion of them.

Mr. HALE, of King's Walden, has cultivated them four years; he sows them the latter end of May broad-cast; hoes them twice always, picks charlock by hand, and uses

---

* This man's land must be a very light barley land.—*H.*

all

all for sheep and lambs; they have been very valuable indeed. In the spring, 1800, he could have sold the crop, eight acres, at 10l. per acre. In the beginning of March, common turnips being over, 200 sheep, and 200 lambs, and 140 other sheep, were kept on them near seven weeks. The same field was to have been sown with barley, and ploughed twice, but being late, was sown with Swedish turnips again, and the crop, without manure, except two cart-loads of pigeon's dung, was in every respect as good as the other. This year the land was ploughed once, and sown with white oats, and the crop was equal to full eight quarters per acre. Last year he had fifteen acres, and this year eleven, of this root. Mr. ROBERTS, the steward, who has a farm himself, has nine acres this year, and intends never to be without them; being perfectly convinced that they are a most useful crop.

I have not seen many finer crops than Mr. HALE's, and all the parts of a full yellow colour.

Mr. BATTEN and Mr. BLINDEL, of Welwyn, both informed me that these roots have been often sown, and for some years past, at Welwyn, but with very little success. The latter thinks none of the land is good enough; but the former has had them on very good and well-manured fields, yet without success. Two years ago he had a miserable crop upon four acres and a half, and when his other turnips were done, his shepherd proposed feeding these, thinking they might last the flock for a few days: they turned out, however, much better than was expected, and kept eight score sheep three weeks; and the sheep were so fond of them, that the shepherd could, after barley sowing, scarcely keep the flock out of the field. The barley was a very great crop.

Lord CLARENDON has five or six acres every year, and finds them of capital use. His Lordship sows in May, on land upon which, in autumn, the dung was ploughed in, as he thinks it very essential for this crop; he stirs the land in April, and ploughs it in May for sowing : he sows three pounds per acre : they are hand-hoed twice; he first uses them in the beginning of March : he did not eat them last year until the 24th April, and had a large barley crop after them. They run very much to top, more than common turnips ; and if his Lordship had none, he would buy them for the spring at a much greater price than common. He feeds first with ewes and lambs, and then store-sheep follow and eat clean. Good barley always grows after them. He has only gravels to sow them on.

These turnips are just coming in at Rickmersworth.

They have a notion at Wheathamstead, that these roots impoverish the land : it is impossible to say what bad management may not contrive to do.

Mr. PARKER, at Munden, has cultivated them four years : he has twenty acres this year, and had sixteen last year ; and as many the year before. The yellow fleshed turnip is much the best. He sows in May, hand-hoes twice, and has always very good crops. He feeds them on the land with sheep ; and draws them for horses, for which stock they are very useful : he uses them also for beasts of all sorts ; they are of prodigious utility in point of duration, and excellent, late in the spring, for straw-fed beasts. He grows as good spring-corn after them as after common turnips ; but manures for them rather higher than for other sorts. They are best on loamy land ; do well on good gravel ; but, on very sharp gravel, they should not be sown. His twenty-acred field this year, for such an extent, is the finest crop that I ever saw, the Earl of WINCHILSEA's at Burley, alone excepted ; yet this crop is from the second sowing in June.

Mr.

Mr. NEWMAN HATLEY has none, as he thinks the land at King's Langley not good enough for this plant.

I saw several large pieces of them on the rich sands between Hoddesdon and Ware; but not of a size equal to the quality of the soil.

Mr. CALVERT, at Albury, has had them four years; has now seven or eight acres: he sows them at the end of May; and finds that there is not any thing so good for every animal for which he has tried them. He once gave a few to some fatting wethers that were at common turnips, and after eating them, they would not take again to the common turnips without much starving. He has had Swedish turnips and common turnips on each side of them in the same field, and sheep turned into the field would not touch the common turnip, but seized on the Swedish immediately. The yellow fleshed is much superior to the white; and the rough coated to the smooth skins. His present plan is, to assign two fields, well situated for the cattle and sheep, and to have one every year under Swedish, and the other in common turnips, to follow each other, by which means no inconvenience will result from not getting the Swedish off in time for barley.

Mr. HILL, of Whittle, thinks they injure the land; by late keeping and running to seed.

Mr. FOSTER, of Royston, has a high opinion of them; and observes that they are peculiarly valuable in a chalk district, where turnips *must* be fed very early, or the barley crop lost: Swedish then come in when most wanted.

From this detail, it is sufficiently evident that the cultivation of the Swedish turnip is thoroughly introduced into the husbandry of this county, and not likely to be neglected in future. The farmers have great merit, in so soon adopting a new plant. It already makes a considerable figure.

figure. Where the soil is not sufficiently rich, it may probably give way; but as to the more common objection of some, that barley cannot follow, not to speak of the success with which so many others sow that grain, it may be observed, that the right system, where the objection has really some foundation, is hinted at in the preceding notes : common turnips, winter tares, or buck-wheat, may properly succeed ; and this double fallow can scarcely fail of answering in the uncommon degree of cleanness, which must be the consequence. Another plan is, to draw such as would remain too late, and strew them on grass for cattle or sheep. The objection, is therefore, in any case, easily remedied.

SECT. XIII.—CABBAGES,

ARE largely cultivated in the experiment ground of the Marchioness of SALISBURY. The seed was procured from Sir WILLIAM GORDON, of Leicestershire, and I therefore concluded that it was from that eminent cultivator BAKEWELL, who had an excellent sort: Sir WILLIAM was his landlord. Lady SALISBURY's are spring sown, and planted out about three feet row from row, and two feet plant from plant. I have rarely seen finer crops. There are many rows of the red cabbage, which is preferred by Mr. STEPHENSON, the bailiff, who thinks that if the best sort of red cabbage were procured, which comes to a very large size, it would beat all others. An acre of prime cabbages is, in consumption and value, fully equal to one acre and a half of prime turnips. They are found chiefly applicable to feeding cows, and the milk and butter are perfectly sweet, with no other attention than that of
freeing

freeing them from all decayed leaves. The cows do well on them, without any hay, and give, while thus fed, a great deal of milk.

Mr. CHAPMAN, of Hitchin, cultivated the great Scotch sort on a loamy soil for sheep: he got great crops; and is clear that his sheep improved as much in one week on cabbages as they did in two on turnips. He did not continue it, because the depredations of the poor people were so great: in any other situation he would never be without them.

Mr. HALE, of King's Walden, has for many years cultivated the large cow-cabbage. He fallows and manures as for turnips. Sows the seed in the spring; plants in June or July, according to the season, in rows a yard square every way. They are kept clean by hand-hoeing. He begins to use them when the cows are taken into the yard, and they are given night and morning with hay to the cattle, and are much more productive than turnips, and answer far better for cows. Some have been given to ewes and lambs, which do exceedingly well; and the hogs always seem very eager to eat whatever is left. In regard to expense, it does not exceed that of turnips. The quantity grown is usually from two to four acres and a half. His crop this year I found fine, and very clean: I think it would have been larger in rows at a distance of three feet from row to row, and had the plants been only from 20 to 24 inches asunder in the rows, instead of 36 from plant to plant.

At the Hoo, I perceived that Mr. BRAND has cabbages: I was unlucky from his absence, and from that of Mr. BROWN also, his bailiff.

Mr. BATTEN, at Welwyn, cultivates them for his

HERTS.] cows,

cows, and finds that they give more and much better milk, and butter, than turnips.

Lord CLARENDON cultivates them for various purposes, with much success; and has a great opinion of the husbandry.

Mr. CALVERT, at Albury, cultivated the great drumhead for some years; but when Swedish turnips came in, he found them preferable, and gave up the former.

Much of the land in Hertfordshire is so well adapted to this crop, that I am rather surprized it has not become more common: these experiments are remarkably in favour of this culture.

―――――

SECT. XIV.――CARROTS.

I FOUND some acres in complete cultivation in the experiment ground of the Marchioness of SALISBURY; and the crop very fine. In the consumption, Mr. STEPHENSON, the bailiff, thinks they answer best for milch-cows: two bushels a day are given the cows: the benefit of thus feeding, however, must depend on situation, for where they can be sold at such high prices as are common near London, cows are thus supported at too great an expense. If the object is viewed in another light, and the prime cost of raising the crop be only considered, then carrots may answer better than hay, and they give far more milk. In the same field her Ladyship has had as far as 640 bushels an acre over four acres*.

Mr. CHAPMAN, of Hitchin, has had two acres, which succeeded greatly; he gave them to horses, and sold many: some others raise them for horses: they are much approved; but the quantity is not considerable.

* I have myself had forty-five tons on five acres; and several carrots of this crop weighed three pounds; four weighed together fourteen pounds.—*H.*

SECT. XV.—PARSNIPS.

THIS plant makes a great figure in the experiment ground of the Marchioness of SALISBURY: the crop is good, and quite clean. Fatting oxen consume them most advantageously: their benefit thus applied, is so great as nearly to equal, in the opinion of Mr. STEPHEN-SON, oil-cake: they are consequently excellent for all stock, but superior in fatting bullocks.

SECT. XVI.—BEETS.

THE common red beet, and the root of scarcity, are cultivated successfully in the experiment ground of the Marchioness of SALISBURY: the former answer greatly in fattening cattle, almost as well as parsnips, and better than carrots.

SECT. XVII.—CLOVER.

THIS noble plant, the introduction of which has wrought a greater improvement in English agriculture than that of any other, has been cultivated in this county, proba-bly as long, or longer, than in any part of the kingdom ; and it yields, from its vicinity to the Capital, a greater profit here than is commonly experienced elsewhere.

Ware.—The best farmers mow the first growth, and always feed the second: they consider it as good ma-nagement to mow the first, as it is, in their estimation, bad to mow the second. However, I saw several second crops

in

in full blossom between Walkern and Stevenage, of a luxuriance that spoke no bad management : nor is it a point
at all ascertained. The practice of various other districts
are in favour of mowing both.

Mr. WHITTINGTON has no doubt upon this point,
thinking that better wheat will be after two mowings than
after one.

Mr. KEATE and Mr. STEPHENSON, at Hatfield, assured me that all that vicinity has cultivated clover so
long and so repeatedly, that the soil is, as the farmers say,
sick of the plant. It matters not how fine a crop may be
in autumn, it dies off in the winter gradually, so that little
is left in May ; and it dies even so late as in that month.
Mr. KEATE had a proof of the benefit of not sowing it
in one or two courses consecutively Having part of a
field for five or six years under lucerne, when it was
broken up, barley and clover were sown over the part
which had been under lucerne, and also on a contiguous
piece where the clover husbandry had not been interrupted ;
on the latter the clover in 1801 failed, and was ploughed
up ; but where the lucerne had grown, the clover was, as
I saw, extremely fine, thick, and regular. This shews that
other grasses may be substituted, and yet the land refreshed,
and prepared for future clover without a failure. The
great price which hay has yielded of late years, has been
an injury to the land ; the farmers have been unwilling to
vary the course, or to plough up a bad plant ; and very
foul fields are the consequence.

Mr. YOUNG, of Hurral, finding clover crops apt to
fail, he sows trefoil also: mowing with him gives better
wheat than feeding. This variation of trefoil is excellent
management.

Mr. CLARKE, of Sandridgbury, has had no clover
fail till last year (1800). If he intends feeding, he mixes
trefoil,

trefoil, otherwise he sows clover alone. He mows some twice for hay ; some once, and then feeds sheep on the land. His best wheat is after two mowings, one for hay, and the second for seed : this he attributes to the great fall of the leaf, and to the plants covering the soil from the sun so well and so long.

Mr. BIGGS, near St. Albans, grows better wheat after mowing than after feeding ; and better after two mowings than one ; and this general superiority has, in his opinion, amounted to four or five bushels an acre.

Mr. WANGFORD, at Bushy, reaps better wheat after mowing than after feeding the clover.

The same observation is made about Berkhamsted, Hempstead, and Beachwood, on whatever soil it may be. At the last-named place, they sow fifteen or sixteen pounds with the barley ; and mow that twice. The average crop amounts to one load and a half for the first, and to one the second : much land is quite sick of it ; when it fails, they sow pease.

Better wheat grows about Hitchin after mowing than feeding : they sow twelve to fourteen pounds : Mr. CHAP-MAN adds six pounds trefoil.

Mr. ROBERTS, of King's Walden, has found that when it has been twice mown, better wheat follows it than when it has been fed.

Mr. BLINDEL, of Welwyn, admits the same fact, but observes, that the reason is in the clover's being fed too close : were it kept to a considerable growth before it were turned in, so that all should not be eaten, but enough trod down to cover the land from the sun, then feeding would give the best wheat.

About Gorhambury, the first cutting amounts to one
load

load and a half; the second to one. Feeding is reckoned
to give the best wheat.

Mr. SEDGWICK, &c. of Rickmersworth, sows twelve
pounds: he mows twice; and mowing is followed by the
best crop of wheat.

The Hertfordshire experience of the superiority of mowing to feeding (for that is the general fact, notwithstanding
some exceptions), coincides with many remarks carefully
made in various parts of the kingdom.

SECT. XVIII.—TREFOIL.

" THE Hertfordshire farmers have found by experi-
" ence, that the succession of clover, their best and most
" valuable meliorating green crop, has hitherto been too
" quick on one and the same field, where the rotation
" has been as follows, viz. wheat on clover lay; oats,
" turnips on a fallow of course; and barley with clover
" seeds; the clover cut twice, or the second crop fed off.
" In every part of a county where the soils so widely
" differ in one and the same field, and where almost every
" species of manure is procurable and used, this failure of
" the clover crops is certainly not imputable either to the
" soil or the culture. Whether Nature requires a longer
" interval of time to recruit the species of nutrition pecu-
" liar to the nourishment of different seeds and plants, or
" to what other cause this failure of clover crops is to be
" attributed, which are sown to give an interval of rest
" between crops of white corn, are questions, in my ap-
" prehension, still involved in uncertainty. I did observe
" this year (1794) very different crops of clover on nearly
" the same soils, in different and distant parts of the coun-
                                                    " ty

" ty of Hertford; in the mixed soils, on the top or apex
" of a chalk pillar, surrounded by strong, shelvy, clay
" land, the clover had missed; a whole patch, containing
" three or four poles of land, was bare, and the sur-
" rounding clover tolerably good. This I imputed to the
" dryness of the season. In other parts I have seen simi-
" lar spots carry the best crop of clover; and, in general,
" where the clover had missed or failed on most soils, it
" had missed or failed in patches, and the rest of the crop
" was tolerably good; which induced the growers to let
" the clovers stand for a crop, and not break them up,
" and sow another crop; though they were aware that
" where they had no clover, they would have little or no
" wheat the succeeding year, as the ground there would
" be beggared by weeds. I saw a crop of clover, in the
" parish of Sheephall, near Stevenage, on strong clay
" land, lying to a good aspect and drainage, and ploughed
" in (three-step) lands about nine feet wide, with deep
" furrows between them. The plant on the lands was
" in most places but indifferent, though on a good hold-
" ing soil; and in the bottom of the furrows it was most
" luxuriant, and overtopped the rest:—here the plant had
" certainly most moisture, but it might possibly have got
" hold of a maiden soil; for this species of clay is good
" productive soil to the centre, if it holds so far; and
" when taken from depths of 50 and 60 feet, and ex-
" posed a short time to the air, it will produce most lux-
" uriant crops. Mr. WHITTINGTON, an excellent and
" improving farmer, who holds a large farm in this pa-
" rish, chalked. about four years ago (1790) land in the
" neighbourhood, and of the same sort with the above;
" and part of it bore a most luxuriant and even crop of
" clover *."

* First Report.

Mr.

Mr. Hog, near Barkway, this year (1801), mowed trefoil for seed, which was immediately thrashed; and the straw he mixed in stacking with meadow-hay about half made: it is now excellent; had he fed the trefoil, it might have been worth 20l. but the seed paid him, perhaps, ten times as much, besides the value of the hay. This is a hint that may be worth attention, to those who put a small value on trefoil straw.

SECT. XIX.——RYE-GRASS.

Very little rye-grass is mixed with clover, for as the best hay goes to London, where pure clover being preferred, the farmers are cautious of any mixture. Mr. Byde objects to it on another account—the fault of the culture is its running to natural grasses, an evil increased by rye-grass, being itself a common grass, and the seed not always free from other sorts.

Mr. Sedgwick, of Rickmersworth, has a very indifferent opinion of rye-grass, as it fouls the land, in his opinion; nor is the following crop of wheat so good, when rye-grass is sown with the clover.

SECT. XX.—SAINFOIN.

Much sainfoin has been raised on Mr. Whittington's farm, but he has none at present; nor does he think of re-sowing it yet, as he understands and believes that the land should remain some years after breaking up old sainfoin, before the same land should be sown with it again.

The Marchioness of Salisbury sowed five acres with sainfoin,

sainfoin, for an experiment, at Hatfield, on a gravel with a wet bottom. This grass remained five years, but did not succeed. It was then trench-ploughed, and oats were harrowed in, and the crop was great.

I have rarely seen finer sainfoin than some small pieces on Mr. CLARKE's farm at Sandridgbury. The soil is a good flinty loam on a chalk bottom. He thinks the price of corn of late has been too high for this grass to answer on any good soil; but he has a neighbour, Mr. THRALE, another tenant of Lord SPENCER's, who sows it on an extensive scale.

There is an odd idea about Berkhamsted, that ashes wear out sainfoin. Mr. ROOPER says that he has experienced it. It commonly lasts fourteen or fifteen years; but if not carefully preserved from sheep, not more than six or seven.

About the neighbourhood of Hitchin, they sow four bushels, with oats on clean land. It lasts on white land ten years, but on gravel seven or eight years; and produces two loads an acre, while in vigour, and even more, but one and a half on an average. The farmers give it to horses, and break it up with oats, sowing them always on one ploughing.

The Rev. Mr. DOVE thinks that it is more profitable to break it up after six or seven years, as the land will then give better crops than after the moss has impoverished it, as he has known some left fourteen or fifteen. The land will yield it again after ten or twelve years. It should be manured every second year, with 40 bushels of soot, or 60 of peat-ashes.

Mr. SEDGWICK considers this cultivation as the best for chalk hills. Four bushels of sainfoin are sown per acre with barley, after turnips. The grass lasts ten years, and produces sometimes from one quarter of a load to two loads per acre.

acre. He ashes it every second year. It is the best hay to sell or use. They rarely cut it for seed, but know it is beneficial to the crop. It will flourish well on the same land again in three, four, or five years.

Sainfoin succeeds well at Munden, and especially on a soil of an adhesive nature, on chalk: they sow four bushels. This grass lasts seven or eight years, and sometimes longer; and produces two loads per acre. Mr. PARKER broke up a field by a summer fallow, and sowed wheat, which the red worm ate up: he then fallowed the land again, and sowed it with turnips.

He broke up another field for Swedish turnips, and had a fine crop; after which he sowed oats.

Mr. RUSSEL, at Cheshunt, sowed sainfoin 40 years since on a strong gravel, and it answered well; and there are still some plants remaining. Mr. CALVERT, at Albury, knows some plants that are 50 years old.

Mr. DOO, at Bygrave, finds sainfoin advantageous to mow only for five or six years; he then feeds it with sheep three, four, or five years, till it has got a good turf for paring and burning.

SECT. XXI.—LUCERNE.

THIS plant deserves to be found in every parish of the kingdom situated on a rich soil; but unfortunately is scarce every where, a few districts in Kent and Sussex excepted.

At Hatfield I had the pleasure of waiting on the Rev. Mr. KEATE the rector, whose lucerne is particularly mentioned by Mr. WALKER, in his Hertfordshire Report. He had one acre and three quarters broad-cast; but

I found

I found it had been ploughed up some years. Its duration was only five years, the natural grass having then got the better of it. In general, Mr. KEATE was very well satisfied with it, as less than two acres fed ten or eleven horses through the summer, which forms a produce, of the profit of which there can be no doubt ; and when it is contended, as it often justly is, that horses devour the produce of immense tracks of land, it should be considered at the same time, that this quantity of land might be very considerably lessened by means of such articles of culture as are well adapted to the keeping of this animal. Mr. KEATE thinks his lucerne in the broad-cast culture would have lasted much longer, but the soil, though a good loam, worth 20s. per acre, has too cold and wet a bottom to suit the plant. It is hollow-drained, a sign that the soil is not fit for it. When the grass was broken up barley was sown, and the crop was immense.

The Marchioness of SALISBURY has in her beautiful experiment ground, three acres of lucerne, in rows at fourteen inches, perfectly clean, and in fine order : I saw it in its third growth, in August, two feet high ; it is two years old, and makes a very fine appearance. In its consumption by horses, I found some doubts of its value, which had not, in 35 years experience and information, ever occurred to me before. The men seem to think that it purges horses too much, and sometimes gripes them ; perhaps arising from inattentive feeding ; leaving too much to heat in the cart, or from some unknown cause.

Lady MELBOURNE had lucerne in drills, which lasted nine years, and produced crops to her satisfaction. Her Ladyship's present crop is four years old ; it is cut four times every year. The rows are eighteen inches asunder ; but the soil being a gravel, and part of it sharp and *burning*, the produce does not exceed that of feeding a horse per

acre

acre through the summer. Her Ladyship intends to sow some more on a better soil, and at twelve inches.

The Rev. Mr. Dove cultivated lucerne at Lilly for ten years, both broad-cast, and drilled at ten inches distance, and also transplanted: the transplanted was the worst; the drilled at ten inches good; but the broad-cast was the best: he cut it thrice a year, and could have done it four times in a favourable season. He gave it to horses and cows, and it answered very well for both.

Mr. Hale, of King's Walden, cultivated lucerne: the first sowing was ate up by the fly; then the land was sown with turnips, and after the turnips, tilled; it was sown again with lucerne broad-cast in May, in order to save it from the attack of the fly: eight gallons of barley were sown with it on two acres, which produced fifteen quarters and a half, and half a peck. The lucerne never grew so as to be worth continuing: it was mown three times the first year, but the three were not equal to one good cutting of clover; he therefore ploughed it up, and sowed oats. The soil was not good enough for this plant; the staple was too thin.

It is sown broad-cast near St. Albans, but on a small scale; and has generally answered very well.

Mr. Doo, at Bygrave, has a field of ten acres broad-cast, which is at present ten or twelve years old. He gave the land (a strong loam on a chalk bottom) a complete summer-fallow, on which he sowed barley half seeded, or two bushels an acre, and the lucerne twelve pounds an acre with it: he regularly mows it thrice a year, and feeds 23 horses with it from May-day to Michaelmas. He sows 50 bushels of soot per acre upon it every year, at 1s. per bushel, having previously harrowed it completely in March, with a heavy drag-harrow, as much as six oxen can well draw; and this across the field in various directions,

tions, till the field has the appearance of a summer-fallow.
He has a very high opinion of it; and esteems it to be excellent for horses, and better than tares, except for a very
short time while they are in full bloom: he can drive or
ride horses 40 or 50 miles a day on it without any inconvenience. It never gives them a looseness. He intends breaking it up in a year or two, but not till he has got another
field laid down with lucerne. To estimate this food only
at 3s. 6d. a week, it amounts to 4l. 0s. 6d. a week for 23
weeks, or 92l. 11s. 6d. for 10 acres; or above 9l. per
acre: a very ample and profitable crop, notwithstanding
the expense of an annual dressing. It may not be improper to remark, that the 50s. an acre in manure, would,
for this plant, be far better expended in rent for land of a
proper degree of natural fertility; and this shews, like so
many other circumstances, how small an object rent is,
when fertility is proportioned to it.

SECT. XXII.—TARES.

In the heavy land districts, I found tares very generally
cultivated for soiling the teams; a husbandry that cannot
be too much commended. It appears by the writings of
ELLIS, that this branch of agriculture was common in
Hertfordshire above 60 years since, before it was at all
practised in many other counties; and I was glad to find
it held its place steadily in the management of the present
period.

Mr. LEACH manures for tares, and if they are mown
early, and three earths are given to the land, he gets good
turnips after them.

They

They are universal at Rickmersworth and Watford; and many are fed off by sheep.

The preceding notes are few, because I found the culture universal in the county; and registers would have been no more than repetitions. Every farmer, at least nineteen in twenty, have tares for soiling their horses. It is one great feature of Hertfordshire merit, being more general than in any other county with which I am acquainted; nor can it ever be recommended too strongly.

SECT. XXIII.—OF THE DRILL HUSBANDRY.

THE drill husbandry would furnish an ample field for experiment and speculation, were a County Report the proper vehicle of general remarks. When the kingdom has been well examined, and the particular experiments of individuals willing to communicate their practice, collected, the subject will probably be well understood: at present it must be considered as unascertained. Hertfordshire, though a tillage county, has but little to offer towards forming a general mass of experience, so very earnestly to be desired on this head in particular, and which, when collected together, would be attended with such beneficial effects.

At Westmill I had passed near 100 miles in the county, inquiring for drilled crops, but neither seeing nor hearing of any. Mr. GREG had tried, but gave it up as unprofitable on this soil.

Mr. BULLOCK, of Bennington, tried the drill-husbandry for several crops: for two seasons he executed the
work

work well, but gave it up from finding his soil improper for it.

The following conversation took place relative to the drill-husbandry, between me and Mr. MARSH, of Simmonside, who made me the following answer to a question I asked, whether he drilled his corn?

—*" No : I have seen enough of it. I will shew you pre-*
" sently as much barley as can grow out of the earth, broad-
" cast, and the land clean : what should I drill for ?"

Lady MELBOURNE, at Brocket-Hall, is one of the principal drillers in the county, where, however, this husbandry is very little practised. Her method is that of Mr. DUCKET, of whose implements her Ladyship has a complete set for this culture. Mr. HAZARD, the bailiff, shewed me several of the crops and stubbles ; the rows straight, the land clean, and the husbandry, upon the whole, practised with intelligence and success : the barley and wheat are sown at a distance of nine inches ; the pease at eighteen, and the turnips last year at twenty ; but she intends to sow the turnips at twelve : this year they are broad-cast. The barley is horse-hoed once, the wheat twice. They sowed near three bushels of barley : last year exactly three were sown, and some crops produced seven quarters an acre, though the soil is not of the first quality. The clover seed is sown in the same drills with DUCKET's clover-drill ; and I saw some that was clean and fine, though part *burning*, from the sharpness of the gravel. Her Ladyship has two farms, one of lighter loam, on a gravel ; the other of strong land. The drilling is chiefly practised on the former. For horse-hoeing cabbages and pease, here is a small double plough, turning a furrow on each side at once : the beam double, and shifting from each other at pleasure, by which means it can be applied to turn two furrows *from* a row of plants,

leaving

leaving them on a narrow strip of land; and by closing the beams, it is a double mould-board plough for earthing up two rows at once. It is a good tool, and does credit to the inventor. The earth-boards expand or contract at pleasure. It came from Scotland. Here is also a Scotch turnip-drill, the seed-barrel revolving: this is, I conceive, inferior to the Tweed-side one, which delivers by a stroke given by the wheels.

After Brocket, a long interval ensued before I met with another driller with JOHN COTTON, Esq. at Hempstead, who has practised this husbandry, but not regularly, for near twenty years; but his chief exertions have been in the last five or six years. In 1799 he had six acres of wheat, besides other crops. In 1800 two acres of beans, sixteen of pease, eight of barley, and six of oats. In this year, 1801, he has twenty acres of beans, twenty of barley, seven of pease, and ten of oats. I viewed the beans, and examined the stubbles of the other crops; they were all very regularly and straight drilled; the beans were a great crop, and the rest must have been good: Mr. COTTON estimates the barley at eight quarters an acre. All succeeded well. He has no wheat this year, nor had he any the last, because it is necessary to lay the fields which would have been drilled, dry by *stiches*, or narrow lands. His distances are, for beans and pease twenty-two inches, barley, oats, and wheat, ten. He horse-hoes the two former; but neither horse nor hand-hoes any white corn. I should observe, that Mr. COTTON's soil, though flinty, and some of it strong and wet, yet has not so many stones as many of the fields in this part of the county. The difficulty of drilling beans in February on strong land, as it is called here, Mr. COTTON obviates, by letting the shares of the drill barely touch the ground, and then covering the seed by passing a double mould-board plough between the rows,
throwing

throwing over them a smooth ridge of earth, such as a gardener makes with a hoe. He has had wheat in succession, and also oats ; but this year, after a great crop of beans, he intends to fallow the land. 1 recommended shimming, broad sharing, or scuffling the stubble, harrowing and burning, and putting in wheat ; but the idea did not seem to be satisfactory. This gentleman's drill is simple, and with any common degree of care, correct ; the delivery is by a notched cylinder at the bottom of a hopper. His horse-hoe has great merits for a stony soil.

Mr. JENNENS, of Hempstead, has been a driller these 30 years or more, from whose practice and success Mr. COTTON took such hints as produced the same exertions on his own farm : he neither horse nor hand-hoes any sort of white corn : the drilling and hoeing of pease are the principal objects of his new husbandry.

Sir JOHN SEBRIGHT drilled pease at 20 or 22 inches, with the Kentish single-shared drill, on very strong flinty land, much out of condition ; yet he cleaned it well by horse-hoeing : he sowed six pecks of seed.

Mr. PARKIN, at Dunstable, drills much wheat with Mr. COOKE's drill, at nine inches, and horse-hoes thrice in the spring, which gives it as deep a colour, nearly, as a dressing of soot. He has used this drill three years, and with great success. This year he had 37 acres drilled on a pea stubble. Mr. ANSTY, at Hoghton, the adjoining parish, has done the same for some years, with success : both these gentlemen have a very high opinion of the husbandry for wheat and pease ; but neither of them have been successful with barley or oats. Pease drilled at twelve inches, produced Mr. ANSTY 50 bushels an acre in 1800, after barley, which followed tares and turnips.

HERTS.]   Mr.

Mr. PARKIN thinks that when the season proves dry, the drought is let in too much.

Let no one think me an enemy to drilling, who thus go out of the county for the sake of mentioning successful drillers.

Mr. SEDGWICK last year drilled with COOKE's drill, half an acre of wheat, the rows at a distance of nine inches, in the midst of a broad-cast crop on a fallow: he hand-hoed it twice; the produce was evidently to the eye a greater crop; and he sowed half a bushel of seed less. In consequence of this, he intends this year to drill all his fallows, 25 acres of stony land.

Mr. SALTER, of Rickmersworth, used the same plough last year on sixteen or eighteen acres, with such success, that he means to drill all his wheat this year.

Mr. PARKER, at Munden, has drilled various crops, but laid it aside. He reasons thus: if you plough as he does, nine inches deep, and never take two crops of corn in succession, you are sure to have your land perfectly clean: what is the object of drilling, but to keep land clean? and if that object can be attained without it, the *necessity* of drilling is not very apparent; nor does he conceive that a driller is likely to plough so deep as he mentions, for obvious reasons; and then he conceives that he would lose as much by want of depth as he gains by any other advantages which he may have in contemplation. He has had, at Fletton, in Huntingdonshire, six quarters an acre of wheat through 28 acres, on clover lay harrowed in. Without disparagement to drilling, such a crop, and many thousands of others, he remarks, are sufficient proofs, that depositing the seed at an equal drilled depth, is not *essentially* necessary.

Mr.

Mr. FORSTER, of Royston, uses COOKE's drill plough for wheat, with satisfactory success; he has been in this husbandry seven years. He drills nine inches asunder, horse-hoes twice or thrice, and sows five to six pecks. He has made fair trials, by measuring both land and crop carefully, and never without finding the drill superior to the broad-cast (except this year, when the latter was the best), and near half the seed is saved. He has drilled barley also for several years, but left it off, under a perfect conviction that it did not answer: when a dry season comes, the sun is let into the ground, and the crop lost. Land cannot be thickly covered too soon : much depends on this ; but wheat, on the contrary, likes a dry year best; and the same reasoning does not hold good. This is his way of accounting for it, but whether just or not, the reader may determine: I only report his words and reasons.

Mr. FOLBIG, of Willian, drilled wheat, barley, and oats, upon a soil very proper for drilling ; but the crops for some years not being on the whole so good as the broad-cast, he left off the practice.

Such are the experiments I met with in this county ; and upon the whole, they leave the subject pretty much as I found it: a conclusion, however, is fairly to be drawn, that a method of putting in crops which has failed with several intelligent cultivators, and only partially succeeded with some others, cannot be generally necessary as a means of profit. The observations relative to barley and oats are against the practice. I allude here to nothing done or talked of in other counties, as my business is with Hertfordshire ; and certainly in this county, the experiments made, by no means ascertain that any advantage whatever may really exist ; nor will the point be cleared up in this county, till some capital farmer, by means

of

of drilling, shall exceed the crops and profit which a
YOUNG of Hurral, a WHITTINGTON of Broad-water,
and a Doo of Bygrave, gain by the common
method.

CHAP. VIII.

OF GRASS.

THE quantity of grass-land in the county is extremely small, compared with that of arable land : there is no grass district in it, except a very narrow margin in the south line, in the vicinity of Barnet, which being near to London, is made artificially productive, by means of manures brought back by the hay-carts. Many of these fields let at 40s. 50s. and 3l. an acre ; but no inconsiderable portion of these lands are held by the occupiers of villas, and consequently do not properly belong to any Report, but such as treat expressly of the vicinity of the Capital . the subject is fully explained for the adjoining district of Middlesex, in Mr. MIDDLETON's very able Report of that county.

Wherever the residence of a gentleman is found (and Hertfordshire abounds with their seats), there is a tract of grass kept artificially productive, whatever may be the soil ; the expense of which is not easily ascertained. And on the rivers, the flat bottoms of the vales, in general very narrow, are, as every where else, in natural meadow : these exceptions being made, the rest is arable.

There is a fine range of meadows on the Stort, which reach from Hockerill to Hertford : they would generally let at 3l. an acre ; but some are at rents of favour, of 40s.

From Hertford to Hatfield, on the same river, there is also much meadow, but many of them in a most neglected condition : High Meadow, as it is called, might be an excellent

cellent one, but it is over-run with rubbish, and poisoned like many of the rest, for want of management. Irrigation in this line might be of immense importance, but there are so many mills, that it is impracticable. The remark is applicable to many other meadow tracts : those about Watford and Rickmersworth are mentioned under the article of irrigation.

At Beachwood, grass land pays better than arable. Sir JOHN SEBRIGHT has harrowed to destroy moss, but found no benefit from it, though the moss has been well torn up. Manure should be spread at the same time : if ashes are spread without harrowing, the moss is destroyed, and the grass improved.

The profit of hay may be conceived when it sells well, by Mr. BYDE's selling clover-hay in his yard to jobbers (who take it to London) at 5l. 15s. a load ; and meadow-hay at 5l. while I was there in August.

Hay and straw are carried to London from Bygrave, two miles beyond Baldock, and ashes, soot, and sheep's trotters brought back : this is a vast exertion. The carriage is hired at Stevenage at 25s. for a load of hay, and 12s. for a load of straw.

At Hatfield, Mr. KEATE's hay, to mow, make, cart, stack, and thatch, costs 20s. an acre. The first mown is made in four or five days ; but that mown later is mown in one day, and carried on the next. Four hay-makers are allowed to each scythe.

I have in various places seen the apparatus for securing hay-stacks from rain, which Sir JOSEPH BANKS used, and communicated an account of to the Annals of Agriculture vol. x. pp. 282, 520, where is a plate of it. Mr. SABINE, of North Mims, procured Mr. BROWN's from Mr. JOSEPH JOYCE, sail-maker in Wapping. A cloth 36 feet by 33, fitted up with strings, loops, pullies,

lies, and three pair of guide-ropes, complete except the
scaffold poles, comes to 25l. He gave the hint likewise
to order it with the strings, loops, and seams, to be placed
on the long side of the cloth, and not across.

On *laying down* land to grass, Mr. CHAPMAN, of the
Stamp-Office at Hitchin, a very intelligent farmer, sowed
Dutch clover and rye-grass this year, part of it with barley, and part of it at the same time without corn, and the
former is much the better plant.

Mr. ROBERTS, of King's Walden, laid down some
land five years ago, by sowing at Midsummer on a fallow, Dutch clover, rye-grass, and hay-seeds. It is worn
out, but did well for three or four years.

Mr. PARKER, at Munden, laid down a field on a good
gravelly loam with white clover, trefoil, and hay-seeds,
which held good for some years ; but being worn out, he
intends to plough it, and to begin in autumn to plough
and work it till clean, which may be by July or August,
when he will sow it with twenty bushels an acre of Ayles-
bury hay-seed, at 6d. a bushel, and ten to fifteen pounds
of white clover, and three of trefoil. He avoids corn, on
the principle that even one crop would take something
from the field at the moment when every exertion should
be made to enrich it.

The improvements on grass land by the Hon. GEORGE
VILLIERS, are interesting : his own account will be
most satisfactory to the reader.

" DEAR SIR,

" IN compliance with your further inquiry, I will now
" proceed to give you the best account in my power, of
" my general system of treating about 500 acres, which I
" have in hand, within fourteen miles of London, on the
" borders

" borders of Middlesex and Hertfordshire. I have every
" year drained a certain portion of my land, according to
" the Essex mode of carrying off the surface-water, for
" though this practice is totally unused by my neighbours
" in the same parish, experience has convinced me, that
" dressing a cold tenacious clay, not previously drained,
" is an absurd waste of time, money, labour, and every
" thing most valuable. Having obtained a tolerably dry
" surface, my next object (with meadow-land) is to
" deepen the staple of soil, and this I do by every kind
" of compost carried on it for two or three years together,
" which I find establishes a better sort of grass than dress-
" ing once in three years. When you favoured me
" with a visit, I recollect your expressing a degree of
" astonishment at my mowing new laid down ground,
" instead of following the more general practice of feeding
" it the first year ; but I think that practice must be pre-
" ferable or not, according to the nature of the soil, and
" the object of converting it into grass land. With re-
" spect to the former, I have found that mine being a
" tenacious, stiff, yellow, clay, if I was to allow even
" the treading of sheep the first year after the grass-seed
" is sown, I should fill the surface with receptacles for
" water, and should have very little, if any grass of a
" coarse quality, notwithstanding my drains, because the
" the sheep or cattle would press the clay soil so close,
" that the water could not penetrate into them ; whereas,
" if I shut up my field, suffering the grass to stand till it
" sheds the seeds, I find the following season that I am
" enabled, by giving only a slight dressing, to cut a good
" crop of hay for the London market.

  " With regard to feeding land laid down for rich pas-
" ture, a different system may, I have no doubt, be
                                          " adopted

" adopted with success ; but I now propose to treat only
" of the ground which I have laid down, as being difficult
" and unproductive under the plough.

" It is very advisable to have the ground as clean as a
" garden before the seeds are sown, but I do not recommend
" dressing till the grass is come up in a proper manner, and
" clear of weeds: being satisfied on these points, the se-
" cond year's crop should be supported by a slight fine
" compost ; for if it is dressed very strongly before the
" sward is established, the young grass will be quite bu-
" ried. I lay my land up as rough as possible during the
" winter, and after its having undergone the influence of
" frost, I harrow and plough it repeatedly during the
" month of March, previous to sowing about half the
" quantity of oats or barley (as may best suit the soil),
" that I should do if I intended having a crop of grain ;
" but my object, in the instance on which I now treat, is
" to draw up and shelter the grass-seeds which I sow
" with the grain. I do not reckon on the first summer's
" crop from new laid-down ground, beyond cutting some
" excellent fodder for the winter. With regard to the
" qualities of grass-seeds, I have hitherto met with much
" disappointment, but I now feel more sanguine on this
" point, from the active researches of a seedsman * under
" the special protection of the BOARD of AGRICULTURE,
" who has obtained by infinite labour and attention, all
" the most valuable grasses both for pasture and hay
" ground ; such as, *the crested dog's-tail, tall oat-grass,*
" *meadow fox-tail, meadow fescue, holcus, rough stalked*
" *meadow-grass,* &c. &c. &c. These have all been
" selected and gathered by hand, instead of what may be
" obtained by chance from stables and mews, which are

* THOS. GIBBS and Co. corner of Halfmoon-Street, Piccadilly.

" full

" full of weeds and rubbish, besides being over-heated in
" the making of the hay, to a degree which must affect
" vegetation in the seeds to a great degree.

" Having stated my general mode of treatment of
" grass-land, I now subjoin an estimate on an acre of
" mowing ground, which will, I hope, be found tole-
" rably correct ; it is taken at an average, and situated
" within fourteen miles of London.

	£.	s.	d.
" Rent from 30s. to 40s. - - -	1	15	0
" Tithe from 3s. to 6s. - - -	0	4	6
" Rates per acre, 4s. to 6s. - - -	0	5	0
" Manure average.			
" Three loads per ann. at 2s. 0 6 0 ⎫			
" Back-carriage, 12s. to 0 16 0 ⎬	2	8	0
" Cartage on land, 0 6 0 ⎭			
" Mowing, 3s. to 5s. - - -	0	4	0
" Making, ⎫			
" Carting, ⎬ 12s to 18s. - -	0	15	0
" Stacking, ⎭			
" Thatching, - - -	0	2	6
" Binding, - - -	0	1	8
" Cartage to London, 16s. to 20s. -	0	18	0
" Rolling, bush-harrowing, and picking,	0	2	6
" Fences should make themselves, -	0	0	0
" Bailiff an improper charge, - -	0	0	0
" Incidents included in average, - -	0	0	0
	£. 6	16	2

" Crop.

" Crop.   £.   s.   d.
" Five dozen per acre, at 4l. per load,   -   6   16   8
" After-grass,   -   -   -   -   -   1   5   0

                                           £. 8   1   8

                  " I am, dear Sir,
                        " very faithfully yours,

                              " GEORGE VILLIERS.

" *Hillfield Lodge, March* 22, 1802."

The Author of this Report, when he lived at North
Mims, upon the poor hungry gravel of that district, made
some experiments in laying land to grass, which deserve
to be mentioned here. A field of five acres three roods
sixteen perches, was, in 1767 and 1768, under rye-grass,
and extremely unproductive. In 1769, it yielded pease.
In 1770, he manured it, and planted it with cabbages,
which nearly failed. In 1771 it yielded a crop of oats, of five
quarters three bushels an acre, and fifteen loads of straw,
affording, upon the whole, a profit of 3l. 18s. 8d. per
acre ; and with the oats were sown 60lb. of white clover,
18lb. of trefoil, 24lb. of rib-grass, 30lb. of common red
clover, and 70lb. of burnet ; all of which succeeded remarkably well. These formed a productive herbage till
1775, but after that it was worn out ; the natural sterility
again prevailed ; and moss appeared : to the last, however, it was much superior to the former rye-grass.

In another field of seven acres and a half of the same
soil, wheat was sown in 1768 on a fallow ; and then fallowed again for two years, and sown with grasses in June
of the second year, with 80lb. of white clover, 32 bushels
of hay-seeds, 30lb. of rib-grass, 34lb. of trefoil, 34lb. of
cow-grass, 10lb. of burnet ; and a small quantity of sain-
                                                    foin

foin and lucerne was added. The plants all took well;
but the whole was smothered with weeds, probably from
the hay-seeds. The success afterwards was very indifferent, and afforded no encouragement.

Another small field of an acre and a half was sown with
burnet amongst buck-wheat, in 1769, on a summer-
fallow; and this succeeded to my satisfaction, because it
was good, profitable, and did not fail. I remarked the
progress of the crops, and was well persuaded from every
circumstance, that there is no other crop so favourable for
sowing grass amongst, as buck-wheat.

Four acres of miserably poor blue pebbly gravel, and
springy, were sown with turnips, in 1768, which came
to nothing: barley was next sown on the land in 1769,
and yielded not two quarters an acre. In 1770 sainfoin
failed, as might have been expected. In 1771 black oats
were sown, and produced two quarters an acre. In 1772
I improved it, and ploughed it into arched lands very
high, and then manured it well with farm-yard dung,
night-soil, and pigeons' dung, at an expense of 6l. an acre.
In 1773 I sowed white oats, which produced five quarters an acre; and with them 32lb. of cow-grass, 32lb. of
white clover, 32lb. of rib-grass, and 40lb. of burnet. All took
well. The arched lands drained the field perfectly; by
being laid across the slope, the springs disappeared. The
burnet did well, even at the bottom of the furrows in the
sharp gravel. The field was productive for three or four
years; then became a good sheep pasture, but the plants
wore out gradually.

Another field of four acres three roods five perches,
of the same soil nearly, but rather better than the preceding, had been under natural grass miserably broken
up for oats in 1770, and bore a very poor crop. Clover
was sown with them (an uncommon husbandry), but
succeeded

succeeded well. In 1772 I sowed oats. In 1773, potatoes, well manured, were planted on the field, and produced
near 400 bushels per acre. In 1774 the land produced
four quarters and a half an acre of barley, with the barley
seed; also 40lb. of white clover, 40lb. of cow-grass, and
32lb. of rib-grass had been sown. All succeeded perfectly
well; and were good for two years; after which I knew
not their fate.

On nine acres, the worst field upon that bad farm, for
which I was offered 3s. 6d. an acre, in 1769 I sowed
oats, after three years miserable rye-grass. The crop was
trifling: I sowed with them 200lb. of common clover, and
160lb. of burnet: they took pretty well, and for two years
were profitably productive, but declined much afterwards,
till I manured it with night-soil.

These trials convinced me that, relative to pasturage,
such miserable soils will agree better with burnet than the
other plants sown; for white clover, trefoil, rib-grass, cow-
grass, &c. all wear out in two or three years. At that
time I was not in the habit of sowing the native grasses of
the soil, which I have since done in Suffolk, on soils upon
which also the above-named plants wear out; yet these
grasses endure well. But the experiments I made may be
of use, in preventing any person trusting for duration in
this district to the plants which I have named. All these
grasses will wear out after two years; they should be
ploughed out then.

On the breaking up of land.—In 1801, Mr. PARKER,
of Munden, ploughed up a grass layer of six or seven
years lay, about nine inches deep in the winter; and
ploughed it twice more before turnip sowing; the second
time he ploughed it across, and strongly harrowed it. The
first turnip sowing failed, which he attributes to his using
old seed; for this year, wherever he used old seed he failed,

and

and succeeded every where with new. He re-sowed the field, and I viewed the crop, and found them very fine. After this crop he will sow barley and red clover, and then wheat. This experiment affords a useful hint in breaking up lands supposed to abound with the red worm.

CHAP. IX.

ORCHARDS.

IN the south-west corner of the county, and particularly in the parishes of Rickmersworth, Sarret, King's Langley, and Abbot's Langley, Flaunden, Bovington, and partly in Watford and Aldenham, there are many orchards: apples and cherries are their principal produce. Every farm has an orchard; but the larger the farm the smaller the orchard. Orchards are found chiefly in farms of from 20 to 50 acres. The apples are most profitable; but cherries very beneficial to the poor, in the quantity of employment which they require in gathering the crop, for which the poor are paid from 4d. to 8d. per dozen pounds. In ten years after planting, cherry-trees begin to bear: each tree should have nine square perches of land. A full-grown tree will produce 50 dozen pounds in a good year; and from 10 to 20 years, six dozen: prices vary from 10d. to 3s. a dozen. The caroon and small black are the favourite sorts. The Kentish will not thrive here at all. None of the apples are for cyder; they sell for 1s. 6d. to 8s. the basket, or bushel: a tree produces from two to 25 bushels. The orchards, whether of cherries or apples, should be under grass and fed with sheep; mowing the hay is so bad for the trees, that some orchards which were very productive while fed, have produced nothing after

a few

a few years mowing.   For ten years after planting, great care should be taken to keep the trees from the sheep, as their rubbing injures them.   No orchards are worth above 4l. per acre.   They rarely exceed four or five acres, as I am informed.

CHAP. X.

WOODS.

THE woods in the country between Hockerill, Ware, and Buntingford, are rented generally at about 12s. an acre, and cut at twelve years growth, when the produce is about 9l. an acre. The Marquis of SALIS-BURY, on a poorer soil, has 1500 acres, that do not yield above 7s. an acre.

There are large tracts of woodland to the south of Hertford, towards London ; 2000 acres almost together. When let to tenants, they are cut at nine or ten years growth, that they may be cut twice in a 21 years lease , but they are mostly in the landlord's hands, and then cut at 12 years. At 12 years they produce from 4l. to 12l.: they are chiefly applied to the making of faggots, except the sallow and willow, which make hurdles.

Mr. ROOK, of Hertford, has hollow-drained many acres, and found it a very capital improvement.

That gentleman estimates that the timber, if well managed, should at every cutting of the underwood produce as much as the sale of the coppice: he makes it a rule to mark every tree himself.

At Beachwood, the best underwood in Sir JOHN SE-BRIGHT's copses is black sallow, superior to all the rest ; of this hurdles are made : hazel and ash are in the next estimation. When black sallow abounds, an acre at 12 years growth is worth 15l. paying better than the adjoining arable land, without including the timber that is taken ;

but

but this is particularly valuable. Wherever Sir JOHN cuts down a timber tree in a copse, he plants a black sallow set, not a cutting, as that will not grow; the sallow takes well, and thickens the wood consequently with the most valuable of the copse tribe.

About King's Walden, the woods let at 10s. an acre.

Lord GRIMSTON, at Gorhambury, lets his woods at 8s. 9d. but his Lordship has much timber in them.

At the Earl of CLARENDON's, at the Grove, ash, elm, beech, larch, silver fir, and Spanish chesnut, thrive best. For a copse, the last excels, and is far beyond the black sallow. Birch, as underwood, is good, and on all soils, from a rock to a bog. In cutting copses at twelve years growth, the beech are left for a second fall, being always cut at 24 years. These woods are let at 9s. an acre, but full of timber, which adds about 5s. to the annual rent. On low ground, alders succeed, which are bought by turners and patten-makers. Beech is burnt for charcoal.

When I consider the immense number of crates, and similar wooden packages for heavy goods, required in London, I am surprized that the woods of Hertfordshire should not pay more.

At Panshanger, in Lord COWPER's grounds, is a most superb oak, which measures seventeen feet in circumference at five feet from the ground, taken from the S. E. by E. side. It was called the Great Oak in the year 1709: it is very healthy; yet grows in a gravel surface, apparently as steril as any soil whatsoever; but it undoubtedly extends its tap root into a soil of a very different quality. It is one of the finest oaks which I have seen, though only twelve feet to the first bough.

Much of the timber in Moor-park is of great antiquity; and no inconsiderable portion of it is in a state of decay: I know not any place where a large quantity of very old
                                                    pollards,

pollards, mixed with many fine and stately trees, and some woods of young and thriving timber, unite better to form masses of a deep impenetrable gloom ; and the ground being waved into bold inequalities of surface, lofty enough to command all the surrounding fertile country, forms upon the whole a place as beautiful as can be found without water ; for the reigning gloom of the wood is a happy circumstance so near London. The boundary fence rarely appearing, one might easily imagine it to be the centre of a vast forest.

In the Duke of BRIDGEWATER's park at Ashridge, the timber is in great quantities ; and many of the beech and oak of vast size.

I have rarely seen finer trees than at Sir JOHN SE-BRIGHT's at Beachwood : it has the name in strict propriety, for the number of stately beeches is great ; but the soil agrees with all sorts of trees : the cedars are immense ; the oak very large ; the ash straight and beautiful ; the larch, spruce, and Scotch fir equally fine, but the beech uncommon. This wood is applied to the use of turners ; and since this war, very much to barrel staves for dry goods. It was formerly 7d. a foot; now 1s. 2d. Sir JOHN has sold oak at 6l. a load, without top or bark.

Lord GRIMSTON sells his oak naked at 5l. to 6l. 5s. the load ; and a load gives fifteen yards of bark, three yards broad, and a yard high, which sells for 3s. 6d. a cubic yard, and costs 6d. in labour.

Mr. SEDGWICK, of Rickmersworth, thinks it bad management ever to let woods to a tenant, as they never will nurse up timber in the manner a proprietor will do.

CHAP.

CHAP. XI.

WASTES.

THE quantity of waste land in Hertfordshire, compared with that in most other counties, is very inconsiderable. There are some small commons scattered about the county, which would pay well for improving, but the quantity is no where very great. The most are near Berkhamsted. In going to the Duke of BRIDGEWATER's, I crossed one, there said to contain 1500 acres, which would pay amply for improving.

Sir JOHN SEBRIGHT has began an improvement of a quantity of waste common that he had a power of enclosing without an act of parliament, which does him much credit. He has built a good cottage for the overlooker, a barn, has enclosed a stack-yard, now full of stacks, and built a double range of sheds from the barn to the south, open only on that side for cattle-stalls, stables, sheep-yard, &c. &c. well planned and executed. The fields enclosed with quick, and defended by posts and rails, are named as under, and contain the respective quantities affixed to them.

Howe's. This field contains 23 acres: was in furze in 1798, and then broken up by a single ploughing with the great Hertfordshire plough, made very stout, and well fortified, and drawn by ten horses, followed by a man to grub up what roots it left; and only half an acre was done in a day. This expense cannot be estimated at less than 30s. a day, perhaps more; or 3l. an acre. Black oats were

were harrowed in, and the crop was bad. In 1799 it was fallowed, and slightly dressed with dung for turnips—the crop was very fine ; they were eaten on the land by sheep ; and in 1800, nineteen acres of it were sown with barley— the crop was very bad. Clover was sown with it, which crop also was bad. He now intends dibbling it with wheat. On the other four acres spring wheat was sown, and sooted in the spring ; the crop produced five loads an acre. It is ascertained that barley will not do on this sort of new land.

St. Vincent's, containing 24 acres. In 1799 this piece was broken up exactly in the same manner as the other, and sown with oats. In 1800 it was dunged, and fallowed for turnips. In 1801 oats were sown, and were a good crop ; clover was sown among them.

Nelson's, containing 20 acres, was broke up in 1799, by paring and burning, and ploughing twice for turnips ; the crop was bad : this husbandry of ploughing pared and burnt land twice, is uncommon. In the improvements I have examined in various parts of the kingdom, and which have been successful, it has been almost universal to give such land only one shallow earth. In 1800 it was sown with white oats ; which was a fair crop. In 1801 turnips were sown, the field having been previously dunged.

Warren's, containing 18 acres, in 1800 had half of it pared and burnt, and half broke up as before, with the great plough, for want of more hands to pare and burn : the ploughed part was sown with black oats, and the crop was good ; the burnt half with turnips. In 1801 Swedish turnips followed the oats ; and white oats after the turnips : both crops were very good.

Pellew's, containing 20 acres. This piece was also broke up in 1800, half pared with SANXTER's paring plough (of Horse-heath, Cambridgeshire), and burnt for

oats.

oats. The other half was ploughed, as before mentioned, with the great plough, and also sown with oats : both were good crops, but the burnt was the best : the paring-plough did well, and is an excellent tool on smooth land ; although it cuts thicker than the paring spade.

Duncan's, containing 12 acres, was broke up in 1799, with the great plough, as above described, and sown with black oats. The crop was very bad. In 1800 it was fallowed for turnips. In 1801 it was dunged, and sown with turnips again. This is a capital beginning for waste, as it wanted only burning.

Sir Sidney's, containing 10 acres, was broke up in 1801 on one ploughing, and black oats were sown.

Upon the whole, Sir JOHN SEBRIGHT is most decidedly of opinion, that the best way of breaking up such wastes, is by paring and burning: were hands to be procured, he would never do it in any other method. It is not so expensive as a single ploughing ; saves much expense in cleaning by tillage ; the crops are better : and the land is left cleaner. Of this great superiority I saw the proof in a neat stubble, half a piece after one method, and half after the other : the difference was very great indeed.

On the enclosure of Caddington, in 1800, Mr. PICK-FORD, of Market-street, hired on a long lease 509 acres of the heath, at 14s. an acre ; and he has improved it with admirable spirit indeed. After the exertions of only a year and a half, he has but 127 acres to break up, and 50 acres more of the land would have been broken up, could he have got men to pare and burn. Two large new barns have been built, stables for 20 horses completed, and stalls for 50 oxen began ; a large house has been built and inhabited ; a well of 136 feet sunk, and a wheel to draw water by an ass, completed ; a lime-kiln also has been built, and a magazine for the lime filled ; the kiln delivers 100 quar-

ters

ters a week for the land : a garden of above an acre has also been enclosed, twice trenched, and manured with a hundred loads an acre of rich stable dung ; besides which, he is working on a yard. All these together shew much active exertions on the part of Mr. PICKFORD, in which no expense has been spared. The goodness of the crops of this year (1801) are manifest by two large barns completely filled, and by immense stacks. Such an improvement, effected in such a space of time, I never yet beheld.

The only crop I viewed (stubbles excepted) were the turnips and Swedish turnips : and these were very good, notwithstanding the want of rain for the latter ; but soon after I left Mr. PICKFORD, some heavy rains fell in three successive days, which must have been very beneficial to them. This field has a part at present under the heath furze, &c. (part of the 127 acres), and it exhibits the vast effect of paring and burning : I stood with one foot on poor furze, and the other in fine turnips !

The land was pared and burnt early in the spring, and the ashes ploughed in very shallow ; it was then well harrowed, and picked, and the rubbish was burnt, as before ; and then the land was deeply ploughed with six horses, and strongly harrowed again to level it : besides all this, a dressing of dung was ploughed in with the ashes. The whole was finished in time to begin sowing the Swedish turnip as early as the middle of May, and to finish sowing by the end of June. The crop is beautifully regular ; but I have doubts (which I must again express) of the propriety of that second ploughing, and especially so deep as with six horses ; which must have brought up a sour stratum too suddenly. Paring and burning, and dung, I think, should and would have given at least as good, and
perhaps

perhaps a better crop, with only the first earth in the common system of so many other improvers : not to speak of the danger of losing the ashes in such deep tillage. The crop, regular as it is, is not too great to have been produced by one earth ; nor any thing like equal to many in Hertfordshire this year in old land.   I have been apt to consider it almost as a maxim, that very deep tillage given for the first time, should be as long before sowing any crop as circumstances will admit.

One hundred and forty acres of heath were once ploughed in March 1800, with great ploughs that cost 1ol. 10s. each: each plough had eight stout horses, and three men to work it : oats were harrowed in ; and the crop was bad. In 1801 70 acres of it were ploughed once for beans, of which one-third was sown broad-cast, and two-thirds dibbled ; the crop was indifferent, as the soil was too light. The other 70 were sown with pease—a sort called the hedge-pea—the crop was immense, and podded to an extraordinary degree. It is a grey pea, but was nearly white when introduced about ten years ago.

The 130 acres of oats of this year are a very good crop, especially those sown with the black soil. Upon 50 of these acres he harrowed in the oats in a wet time, in order to consolidate the soil, too loose and open ; besides which, he hired from 36 to 50 hands to pick the furze roots, which, as well as the carting them to the amount of 50 loads, was executed after the sowing, and also in wet weather. He is clear that the crop was much improved by this management, and that black oats will not suffer by it.

Mr. PICKFORD has had experience of lime in Cheshire, which induced him to build a kiln here ; he will make it
a capital

a capital experiment; for in all he does, no expense is spared. His kiln is of the diameter of 14 feet at the top, drawn in very little, and 13 feet deep. He burns his lime with coal and breeze, called also *slack*, or small coal.

CHAP. XII.

IMPROVEMENTS.

SECT. I.—DRAINING.

THE importance of hollow-drains is no where better understood than at Sawbridgeworth and its vicinity, upon clay and strong loam. They vary the distance from five to ten yards, and fill the drains with bushes, or with straw; Mr. PARRIS uses long pea-straw in preference, and has tried the twisting it into a rope, which answers perfectly. The expense in labour amounts to 2d. a rod. The effect is so great, that the improvement of the first crop has often paid all the expense.

All Mr. BYDE's strong land is drained; he fills his drains with black-thorn, which lasts 20 years. His workmen dig in three spits a depth of thirty or thirty-two inches, and are paid at the rate of 6d. per pole.

All the wet lands at the Hadhams are very assiduously drained. The same management extends to Buntingford, and thence to Stevenage.

The Marchioness of SALISBURY has done much with the mole-plough, and finds it answer well. Mr. KEATE has also used it; but sufficient attention is not paid in the direction of the drains, which should always be diagonally *across* the slope, and not *with* it.

Mr. MARSH drains much, at the expense of 45s. an acre, at the distance of one perch apart; he ploughs a very deep furrow, and then takes a spit from 18 to 22 inches deep:

he

he has also used the mole-plough with great success, for the drains have stood well five years.   He put only four or six horses, to it, which being far short of eight, ten, or twelve, used in common, I examined his plough, and found it with a gallows and wheels before, raised or sunk in work by an iron ring and chain from the carriage, raised or lowered by an iron pin in holes in the beam, like the great Hertfordshire common plough ; it has also a short roller at the heel; thus the friction is doubly eased : the improvement is very important.

Mr. ARCHER, of Clothall, has tried this plough, but without success: the land proved too stony, and threw the tool out.

Mr. SMITH, of Clothalbury, makes many hollow-drains, nearly a pole asunder ; he ploughs twice, and then takes a spit of 16 inches.

I must observe on this practice of hollow-draining, that I have only named a few instances of persons with whom the conversation turned on this subject ; but it should be observed on the husbandry in general through the county, that there is no part of it within my knowledge, in which it is not well understood and practised.

SECT. II.—PARING AND BURNING.

I HAD little expectation relative to this practice in Hertfordshire ; and in the few cases I found, it was quite of modern introduction : it is, however, likely to spread, and wherever it does spread, *under judicious regulations*, it will be found a most valuable improvement.

In Offley, some sainfoin was pared and burnt; and
wheat,

wheat, barley, and oats sown, but no turnips; they got very good crops two years running, perhaps three : some persons thought it did not answer the expense.

At some distance about Barkway, Royston, and to Baldock, this husbandry has been practised some years, and with great success: many of the men employed of late in the great improvements on Newmarket-heath, came from Langley and Clavering: all round this country it is well known, and highly approved ; nor does any evil ever result from it, except when corn is taken too freely after it. This information was given me by several very respectable cultivators assembled at Barkway, who were all of opinion that the practice itself is excellent; and mischievous only in the abuse.

At Kelshal, adjoining to Therfield, this husbandry has been much practised, as Mr. FORSTER informed me, and that it answered well ; the thin staple of the soil was represented to me as a motive for burning ; and that little else could be done ; and the success justifies the assertion : but they are said not to spread the ashes soon enough. They ought to be spread immediately, and quite hot, by which means Mr. LANE, of Carleton, on 200 acres got seven quarters an acre of barley this year.

Mr. Doo, of Bygrave, who occupies 1000 acres, the largest farm in the county, is a decided friend to this husbandry : the vast exertions he makes in purchasing manures, and his cropping in the four shift instead of the five shift oat course, are proofs that he has no views to exhaust his land. He thinks its advantages or disadvantages depends entirely on the succeeding management; and with proper attention, that it is an admirable system. All the fields which rain would permit me to see of his farm, have been pared and burnt : a sainfoin field he pared and burnt

for

for pease, and got a good crop; I found it ridged up for barley by a third ploughing, and it will have five or six quarters of malt-dust per acre. The fields he could not burn for want of hands, have not answered nearly so well; nor are they in such good order. When he sows turnips for the first crop, he ploughs twice or thrice, and finds it difficult to get the land fine enough, for he has no notion of sowing them on one ploughing.

" Paring and burning, wherever practicable, is evi-
" dently one of the greatest improvements possible, par-
" ticularly on loamy land. On light land, it is less ad-
" vantageous, and very rarely practised, or practicable;
" but in some parts of Herts, they have found means to
" pare and burn old sainfoin lays, and that with great
" advantage; for every farmer knows that these lays pe-
" rish, in length of time, from the superior growth of
" sour grass. As slight reasoning invalidates the propriety
" of this practice, so would deeper strengthen and con-
" firm it *."

SECT. III.—MANURING.

THERE is no part of the kingdom in which this branch of husbandry, every where so important, is more gene-rally attended to; or where exertions in it are more spi-rited. When the quality of the soil is compared with the products it yields, it will be apparent that manuring alone must occasion a disproportion so very great between the soil and the crops; the latter being very superior to the soil. The fossil manure of the district, and the expensive additions from London, are used on a very extensive scale.

* MS. Annot.

Chalk.

Chalk.—" The prevailing practice of sinking pits,
" for the purpose of chalking the surrounding land, en-
" ables me to remark in general, that the basis of the
" soil will be found to consist of a deep bed of chalk ; the
" superstructure, an irregular indenture of chalk and
" earth-pillars ; the earth-pillars broadest at top, and nar-
" rowing as they descend ; the chalk-pillars broadest at
" the bottom, rising conically, and narrowing as they
" ascend to the surface : the chalk-pillars frequently as-
" cend to the surface, make part of the staple, and the
" whole extent of the apex is visible in ploughed lands.
" The earth-pillars have been found to descend 50 feet
" and upwards, to the no small mortification of the chalk-
" pit diggers, who are frequently obliged to abandon a
" pit which they have sunk in an earth-pillar, to the
" depth of 20 feet and upwards, and sink in a fresh spot
" with better hopes of success.

" This general rule admits, however, of many excep-
" tions ; the chalk, in several parts of the county, is co-
" vered for many acres together with a great depth of
" earth, which often renders the question of a chalk basis
" uncertain ; and the downs skirting the county towards
" Cambridgeshire, are for the most part a continued bed
" of hurlock, or bastard chalk, covered with a very thin
" staple.

" The undermentioned method is pursued in chalking
" land, and the persons employed therein follow it as a
" trade : a spot is fixed upon nearly centrical to about six
" acres of the land to be chalked ; here a pit, about four
" feet diameter, is sunk to the chalk, if found within
" about 20 feet from the surface ; if not, the sinkers con-
" sidering that they are on an earth-pillar, fill up the pit,
" and sink in fresh places, till their labour is attended with
" better success. The pit from the surface to the chalk,

" is

" is kept from falling in by a sort of basket-work made
" with hazel, or willow rods and brushwood, cut green,
" and manufactured with the small boughs and leaves re-
" maining thereon, to make the basket-work the closer.
" The earth and chalk is raised from the pit by a jack
" rowl on a frame, generally of very simple and rude con-
" struction: to one end of the rowl is fixed a cart-wheel,
" which answers the double purpose of a fly and a stop;
" an inch rope, of sufficient length, is wound round the
" rowl, to one end of which is affixed a weight which
" nearly counterbalances the empty bucket fastened to the
" other end. This apology for an axis in peritrochio,
" two wheel-barrows, a spade, a shovel, and a pick-axe,
" are all the necessary implements in the trade of a com-
" pany of chalk-diggers, generally three in number. The
" pitman digs the chalk and fills the basket, and his com-
" panions alternately wind it up, and wheel its contents
" upon the land: when the basket is wound up to the top
" of the pit, to stop its descent till emptied, the point of a
" wooden peg, of sufficient length and strength, is thrust
" by the perpendicular spoke in the wheel into a hole
" made in the adjoining upright or standard of the frame,
" to receive it. The pit is sunk from 20 to 30 feet deep,
" and then chambered at the bottom, that is, the pitman
" digs or cuts out the chalk horizontally, in three sepa-
" rate directions; the horizontal apertures being of a suf-
" ficient height and width to admit of the pitman's work-
" ing in them with ease and safety. One pit will chalk
" six acres, laying on sixty loads on an acre; if more be
" laid on, and to the full extent of chalking, viz. 100
" loads, then a proportionable less extent of land than six
" acres is chalked from one pit. Eighteen barrowfulls
" make a load, and the usual price for chalking is 7d. per
" load, all expenses included; therefore the expense of
                                        " chalking,

" chalking, at 60 loads per acre, is 1l. 15s.; and at
" 100 ditto, 2l. 18s. 4d.; as the chalk is considered to be
" better the deeper it lies, and the top chalk particularly,
" if it lies within three or four feet of the surface, very
" indifferent, and only fit for lime, or to be laid on roads,
" gateways, &c. the chalkers must be directed to lay by
" the chalk for the first three or four feet in depth, to be
" applied to the above purposes; if it be not wanted for
" those uses, it is again thrown into the pit when filled
" up. The flints, also, must be picked out from the
" chalk before it shall be carried on the land; for if the
" pit-makers be not narrowly watched, they will chalk
" with both.

" Mr. JOHN HILL, of Coddicot, farms upwards of
" 1000 acres in the adjoining parishes of Coddicot and
" Kimpton, a considerable part of which is his own
" estate; he has chalked many acres of land, and ap-
" proves much of the practice; he chalked a field of
" strong clay land in the autumn of 1793, laid on 60 loads
" to an acre, and the chalk where the pits were sunk
" lay about ten feet from the surface. I viewed this field
" the 7th of August, 1794; it had borne a crop of pease
" since it had been chalked, and was then under the
" plough, preparatory for a crop of wheat: the chalk
" was good, and the land appeared to work well, though
" the chalk was not then thoroughly incorporated with
" the soil. Mr. HILL never lays on more than 60 loads
" of chalk on an acre; this he finds will not only make
" the land work much better, and with less strength of
" cattle, but also, with a light coat of dung, or spring
" dressings occasionally laid on to quicken the vegetation,
" produce abundant crops for ten years; he then chalks
" again, with equal success *."

* First Report.

Mr.

Mr. BYDE has very good chalk at Ware-park : I found a great quantity ready drawn for a light turnip loam, which he intends to lay to grass with barley after the present turnips, and to spread the chalk on the stubble upon the young seeds. He pays for winding it up in buckets, 7d. a load of 24 bushels ; and 8d. a foot for the shaft till the chalk is found : the men will barrow it on to the land, at the distance of 20 poles, for 8d. but then they open a fresh shaft at every 40 yards. They have 2d. in the shilling for beer ; and for filling it into carts and spreading it, 4d. a load more. Forty loads are the common quantity per acre. Mr. BYDE finds that it does more good on his light soils than on the heavy ones ; and conceives that it is apt to subside, and after some years be lost, and that it should be spread at such a period of the cropping. as to be kept on the surface with ploughing as long as the course of husbandry will allow it.

Mr. WHITTINGTON remarks, that chalk used as manure, is, for some time, bad for wheat, though good for every other crop ; and considerably the most useful on land that burns, as gravel : it is of little benefit on cold wet soils. On land subject to sorrel, chalk is a sovereign cure, killing that weed speedily : a circumstance favourable to stock as well as to the soil, for it is very unwholesome for sheep : he has several times lost lambs by their eating it, as it gives them a cholic. He finds fifteen loads of chalk per acre, and repeated once in ten or twenty years, much better than a larger quantity at once. The chalk drawers in this part of the county, will cover eight acres with barrows from one pit in the centre.

Mr. MARSH, of Simmonside, near Hatfield, lays 50 to 60 loads an acre, at 22 buckets or heaped bushels per load, usually in the fallow year, for turnips, and spreads dung on the chalk, which is found to work singularly well with chalk ; but chalk alone does much good for turnips. Upon

HERTS.]   his

his farm, the chalk shafts are fourteen to twenty feet deep. I saw three large heaps drawn ready for laying on.

The chalk about St. Albans and Sandridgbury is hard : Mr. CLARKE lays 50 loads an acre; it is all drawn up in buckets.

Mr. BIGGS, near that town, spreads also 50 loads each of 22 buckets, of one bushel and a half, at 8d. a load, barrowed on to the land; he pays 3d. a foot for the shaft, which is seldom more than six or eight feet to the chalk; the men will do four or five acres from one shaft.

Colonel DORRIEN, at Berkhamsted, carts some hundred loads of chalk, in the autumn, into his farm-yard, to fodder upon, and then mixes the chalk with the dung. Around Berkhamsted, the expense of chalking amounts to 1s. for opening the pit. For a load of 22 barrows, the farmers pay 8d.; for spreading 20 loads, 1s.; for breaking ditto, 8d.; for filling pits, 1s. 6d. for every 20 loads that came out; and they give also small-beer, or 1d. in the shilling on the whole amount : the whole is wheeled on to the land; and generally six or seven acres are chalked from one shaft.

Mr. ROOPER, of Berkhamsted-castle, has found from much experience, that chalk acts with the greatest effect on the flinty, gravelly loams, by *cooling* them, as he expresses it ; but on strong and clay soils, by drying them. It is spread even on soils where the chalk itself is near the surface.

Mr. COTTON, of Hempstead, thinks also, that it does most good on gravels : there is, however, much uncertainty in its effect. He once chalked a field of clay, and it did not bear a good crop of corn afterwards, for some years; but a neighbouring farmer did the same thing, and got a fine crop of wheat the first year; yet wheat is sometimes apt to be hurt, from the chalks being broken up by
                                                              the

the frost, and consequently, by the wheats being rendered light and root-fallen. It is agreed, that land chalked, wants the more dung on that account.

Chalk is much used about Beachwood, in the proportion of from 20 to 40 loads an acre: it lasts ten or twelve years, and does best on wet loamy land; but this sort requires more frequent chalkings than any other. It does well on clay, and lasts longer; and has much effect in making the land plough more kindly.

It is used about Hitchin. Mr. CHAPMAN has chalked on gravel, and with much success: he spread it on a field last year, and sowed turnips, and the benefit was to that first crop so great, as to be seen in the plant to an inch: this was a sharp gravel. He knows a field of strong clay, chalked many years since, in which the improvement is clearly seen at present.

Mr. HALE, of King's Walden, lays 50 loads an acre on clay, and binding flinty land, and its only use is to make these soils work well, which it effects perfectly; 18 buckets here make a load, and contain about a bushel each. It is laid on at the rate of $7\frac{1}{2}$d. per load; and lasts twenty years.

Lord GRIMSTON has chalked his whole farm, having laid on from 40 to 50 loads an acre: it lasts twenty years.

About Rickmersworth, chalk does best on gravelly land, at the rate of 50 loads an acre; a load contains 22 buckets. Mr. SEDGWICK is clearly of opinion, that carting will not answer; he would never cart on any account, as barrowing is so much better. The chalk lasts good fourteen years. It is laid also on the strong clay adjoining Middlesex, and with great success.

At Albury, much of the clays have been chalked, but they say that the only benefit perceivable, is to render them

drier,

drier, that they may be ploughed more early ; and that, in general, they work mellower.

At Clothall, I found Mr. SMITH had chalked a fallow for wheat, at a rate which seemed to my eye uncommonly thick, and found it amounted to 70 loads. He finds it does best on binding loams, composed of clay and sand ; 18 buckets, of near two bushels each, make a load. It lasts fifteen years.

Upon the whole, I must observe, that this husbandry, which is general through the county, has considerable merit; but the great singularity, is the long established practice of drawing it up by shafts, and barrowing it on to the land. Those who have been accustomed to the marle-carts of Norfolk and Suffolk, know what severe work to the teams, that business always proves ; and what a most heavy expense attends it. Horses of great value are often lamed or destroyed, and the purchase of carts and harness, with the wear and tear of both, form very heavy articles. The Hertfordshire custom is therefore much to be preferred. One objection is obvious ; so soft a substance as marle or clay (compared with chalk), could not be trusted to for chambering under-ground, without great danger to the workmen. The discovery of some plan to obviate this, would be of so much advantage as to render it an object of much interest to the public ; nor do I conceive the thing difficult to be effected by moveable arches of timber-work, to be raised as the men advance. A good mechanic would easily contrive such, and the object highly deserves attention: marling and claying would be much promoted among many farmers, particularly small ones, who at present fear to undertake it. Two or three pounds an acre could be easily afforded by men who could not set any regular clay-carts at work for want of a scale of business proportioned to such teams, &c.

Soot.

Soot.—About Stevenage, they spread 20 to 40 bushels an acre, bringing it from London : it costs 8d. and the carriage 3d. in all 11d. per bushel.

Mr. CLARKE, of Sandridgebury, spreads 35 to 40 bushels an acre on wheat.

Mr. WANGFORD, of Bushy, uses 30 bushels an acre on wheat.

About Beachwood, they sow 30 to 40 bushels on wheat in February or March, bought at 1s. a bushel at London; and bring 160 bushels in a waggon with four horses.

Around Hitchin, 40 bushels are sown on wheat.

A great deal is used at Watford, at the rate of 40 bushels an acre.

About Barkway, they have a very high opinion of it ; 50 bushels an acre, brought 30 miles from London, is seen on wheat to an inch.

These are but insulated notes, without the further remark in general, that the practice is universal through the county ; insomuch, that I question whether there is a parish in it, in which some men are not in the habit of using this manure from London.

Lime.—" I know from experience, and it seems uni-
" versally agreed, that chalk lime (and no other can be
" used in Hertfordshire) does not exceed chalk itself in any
" proportion to its expense, so as to give encouragement
" to burn it, unless it be in parts where chalk is far
" distant *."

Ashes.—Mr. BYDE esteems ashes as a manure that acts by opening and loosening the soil, but that they do not feed a crop.

At Little Hadham, &c. they lay on 80 bushels an acre on clover, and pay 3d. a bushel for it.

---

* MS. Annotations, J. HUTCHINSON.

About

About Stevenage, 50 to 60 bushels are given to an acre.

About Hatfield, some lay on 100 bushels per acre, at the rate of 3d. and 3½d. and some very good and well kept at 6d.

Mr. WANGFORD, at Bushy, sows 90 to 100 bushels per acre on clover.

About Berkhamsted their use is universal : generally twelve sacks are given an acre ; the sack contains one bushel heaped, and four struck : the price at present amounts to 1s. 6d. a sack at the wharf; but before the Grand Junction Canal, they cost from 2s. to 2s. 6d. Mr. ROOPER has sent his waggons empty to London, 26 miles, for this manure ; but in general, hay, or beech plank, is carried. Very little clover is to be found, which does not receive the dressing of twelve sacks ; 1d. a sack is allowed for sowing them. They are supposed to last two crops, and to be of such benefit to the wheat, that when a tenant quits a farm, he is allowed half the expense laid out in ashing the clover, which the in-coming tenant sows with wheat. Some few instances are found, of sowing them on wheat. The time is usually January, if the season is mild or moist.

Sir JOHN SEBRIGHT destroys moss in his park by ashes ; but he thinks they do little good to the wheat that follows the clover on which they are spread, otherwise than by improving the clover ; and he is clearly of opinion, that it is better husbandry to soot barley than to ash clover : the soot will do much good to the following clover, whereas the ashes do no more good to the wheat than by increasing the clover. The farmers here sow 10 to 16 sacks on clover.

About Hitchin, ashes are very beneficial, and being spread on the clover, do as much good to the wheat following as a sooting would do.

Mr

Mr. KINGSMAN, at King's Langley, compared ashes sown in November on clover against ashes sown in February; five lands of one, and five of the other; the quantity being equal. Those used in November produced the best crop by about a quarter of a load of hay per acre.

Mr. FORSTER, of Royston, does not much approve of ashes, except on clay to sharpen the soil: they do little good, in his opinion, on arable chalk.

Bones.—This is a manure much esteemed in Hertfordshire; but the price has risen so high of late years, as much to restrain its use. They were formerly 8s. or 9s. a chaldron; but are now 16s. at London. They are considered as best for pastures when burnt; but for arable clay better when only boiled. This manure, especially when the bones are only boiled, is the most durable of those commonly used in Hertfordshire.

Burnt bones are used about Hatfield, *at* 8*d. a bushel.* Boiled, 1l. 1s. a chaldron at Hertford; were formerly 7s. The burnt lasts here four or five years, but they do best on poor land, cold clay, &c. and also on ground lately laid down in grass.

Mr. CLARKE, of Sandridgbury, lays six chaldrons an acre, at 11s. to 14s. a chaldron at London. Three chaldrons are a very heavy load for four horses. He has great doubts about their application: on one field of a strong clay loam, boned eight years since, he still sees the effect to an inch, but in a field adjoining, they have had no perceptible effect; for which he knows not how to account, unless it was caused by a very severe frost, which I do not think probable, as they were in heaps. The same result has attended some other experiments.

Mr. WANGFORD, at Bushy, uses three waggon-loads of boiled on an acre; they last six or seven years.

About

About Berkhamsted they are reckoned to be most serviceable on binding loams.

Bones are used much about Langley and Watford; and are excellent.

Mr. PARKER consuming his hay and straw at home, goes little to London, but when he does, he prefers bones and night-soil to all other dressing.

" Raw bones are the most lasting of any manures.
" Three chaldrons are enough for an acre, and four must
" be allowed to be a great abundance. They enrich the
" ground for many years; and then the mechanical effect,
" in lightening it, will last almost for ever. They may
" be got at many great towns where no manufacture of
" bones is carried on: the best method of using them is,
" to lay them in pretty large heaps, and cover them with
" long dung, whereby the sinews and flesh hanging about
" them will be rotted, and when the ground is ready to be
" ploughed, carry, spread, and plough in the bones im-
" mediately, otherwise they will be carried away by dogs,
" rooks, &c. &c.*"

Oil-Cake.—The best dressing *(compass,* as it is called in Hertfordshire) which Mr. BYDE has ever observed for wheat, is top-folding even so late as May, with sheep fed with oil-cake in troughs.

Rape-cake in dust, is used at the Hadhams, at 20s. a quarter, which is about equal to 6l. 10s. or 7l. per ton. There are mills that grind it at Ware.

Mr. GREG imports large quantities of rape-cake from Ireland; and has attached to his thrashing-mill a stone for grinding it to dust, as a manure, the use of which he much approves.

* MS. Annotations on First Report. J. HUTCHINSON.

Mr.

Mr. WHITTINGTON finds that it answers best when spread on wheat.

Mr. MARSH fats beasts on lintseed-cake for the sake of the manure ; lays the dung on land for potatoes. He fats sheep also on this cake.

Mr. YOUNG, of Hurral, gives his fat wethers chaff, hay, and oil-cake, while they eat turnips on the land; and this is of all preparations the best for barley.

Mr. CHAPMAN, of Hitchin, gave oil-cake last year (1800) to his sheep fatting on turnips, and it answered so well, that he is determined always, in future, to give either cake or corn with that root. He has the new Leicester breed.

Mr. SEDGWICK, of Rickmersworth, has given lintseed oil-cake to fatting sheep and beasts, and it has answered well.

Of rape-dust brought from Cambridge to Barkway, &c. they lay three quarters, or near half a ton, on an acre.

Mr. HILL, of Whittle, always gives oil-cake or corn to sheep feeding on turnips, and is perfectly convinced that it answers at any price at which he has known cake to have been sold. Last year he ground black damaged barley for this purpose; by means of this food the sheep lose no time on putting them to turnips; and go on so much faster than without it, that no doubt can be entertained of the profit ; half the value of the cake is left on the land.

At Barkway, Royston, and Baldock, &c. eleven quarters of rape-dust is called a thousand, and last March cost 20l.; much is used all over that country.

Mr. DOO, of Bygrave, uses great quantities, at 18l. per thousand, and has paid 20l*.

Malt-

---

* Rape-dust is much used in that part of Yorkshire where I reside, between Tadcaster and Doncaster, and as far as Boroughbridge, and in other parts

Malt-Dust.—This is sold at 8s. or 9s. a quarter. At Ware, it used to be 3s. or 4s. a quarter: now it is sold for 11s.

Mr. MARSH, near Hatfield, uses it for wheat, at 12s. a quarter: it works much the best on wet land.

At Hitchin, the farmers use five quarters an acre, at 14s. for barley or turnips.

It is a common manure in every part of the county.

Rabbit-Dung—Mr. CASSMAJOR, of North Mims, has used much of this manure, and with good success, at 2s. 8d. a quarter; but now, since the price has been raised to 3s. 6d. he brings none from London: he spread it for turnips, at the rate of 20 quarters an acre.

Mr. MARSH, near Hatfield, continues to use it at the price of 5s. 6d. a quarter, all expenses included, as I suppose: he spreads it for turnips.

parts of the West Riding also. I have a mill to grind my own rape-cake, that the dust may not be mixed ; and I use a great deal. My mill has saved me a very considerable sum since I erected it. The erection, including the granary over it, cost me 160l. I have paid near 300l. for rape-cake within these eight months. It is certainly best for wheat. I lay on from 12 bushels to 24 per acre, according to the goodness of the land ; or more properly, its condition. Two, three, and four quarters, have been laid on for barley by my neighbours, for which I very seldom use it; never, but for want of other manure: because, when we want rain in spring, and the weather is hot and dry, the manure is not of the least advantage, but loses its goodness from the heat of the weather and the want of rain. Six quarters and two bushels make a ton, but with many dust-sellers, as it is said, seven. I have paid this spring, 5l. 17s. 6d. per ton for ten tons ; and last winter, I paid 7l. and 6l. 15s. The best use to which this manure can be applied, is in the quantity of 12 or 16 bushels per acre, to add to the richness of the soil, already in tolerable condition. I have gained from 10s. to 15s. per ton, and more, by grinding my own cake, besides having it unmixed : and I have the advantage of buying it in cakes at any time of the year ; for as the two seasons for using it come on, it increases in price, and is again cheaper, when they are past. The cake now is not so good as formerly, for the manufacturers of rape-oil now contrive to press the cake twice, whereas formerly they never pressed it more than once ; and they used horses where they now use water, wind, and steam. It cannot be applied as a manure better than for wheat—*H.*

Mr.

Mr. Young, of Hurral, in the same parish, dresses his barley land (if the preceding turnips were not sufficiently manured), with rabbits'-dung, and uses six quarters an acre ; or five cart-loads of hog-dung.

Rabbit-dung is much used about Rickmersworth, for turnips, and they lay 50 or 60 bushels an acre.

Night-Soil.—Of all the manures which Mr. Cassmajor, of North Mims, brings from London, none equal this: he lays three cart-loads an acre, at 10s. 6d. a load, and spreads it dry with a shovel. The effect is great. It is much used about St. Albans.

Since the canal, this valuable manure has been introduced at Berkhamsted.

Mr. Parker prefers this to all other London manures, bringing only bones and felmongers' poke besides.

About King's Langley they bring night-soil mixed with street-sweepings ; a barge-load at 27l. does ten acres. They spread it for turnips; and the effect is greater than that of any other manure.

The Writer of this Report made an experiment on improving a poor, cold, wet, steril meadow, called Rush-Mead, by means of night-soil, which deserves to be mentioned. It contained three acres and a half, and produced, in five years, to the value of no more than 14l. 12s. It was drained in 1769, and, in 1773, that operation being found quite insufficient alone, a small pond was emptied ; and 143 one-horse cart-loads of mud being laid in a heap, seven waggon-loads of night-soil from London were laid on it : the heap was very carefully mixed together, the men being paid by the day. In composts where one ingredient is very rich and the rest poor, this is essential. The men cut a trench through the heap; then threw a small parcel into it, worked it all to pieces, and well mixed it before

fore they threw it up to that part of the heap which had been finished: this compost was spread over the field at the total expense of 12l. 6d. The first produce amounted to 15l. 4s. or more than five preceding years; the second to 9l. 8s.; the third to 12l. 10s.; the fourth to 11l. 10s.: the return was, consequently, ample.

In another field newly laid down in grass, every part proved very poor, except two acres, on which four waggon-loads of night-soil were spread directly, without being mixed with any other manure. The field was fed, and the effect of the night-soil was very great: while the rest of the field never seemed more than half filled with useful plants, this part thickened surprizingly, and grew most luxuriantly; but the cattle, neglecting the rest of the field, were perpetually feeding here; so that, by autumn, it was pared down like a fine green lawn, by the side of a dusky, rough, ragged pasture; which proves that those writers who tell us, vegetables fresh from any rank manure, are ill-flavoured to cattle, much mistake the matter, and have been guided by theory rather than experience. This part of the field continued excellent.

Peat-Ashes.—About Lilly, and the vicinity, these ashes are brought from Bedfordshire, from Tingrith, Fletwick, and Flitton, where they are burnt in heaps, and sold: they were formerly sold for $4\frac{1}{2}$d. a bushel, but now sell for 6d.

" Peat has been found and used in many parts of Herts.
" Sir LIONEL LYDE, at Lawrence Ayot, burnt it into
" ashes for land. J. HUTCHINSON used it for fuel and
" ashes, at Hatfield, as Lord SALISBURY is supposed
" still to do. The sub-stratum was generally gravel: the
" land, after cutting and taking away the peat, became
" sound and good meadow ground; and where the water
" could not so well be got off, osiers were planted. This
                                                    " land,

" land, before improvement, was worth hardly any
" thing; but the peat, as sold, paid about 50l. an acre;
" and the land, drained and laid out for flooding, and
" flooded accordingly, became worth from 50s. to 3l. per
" acre, and was bought, after that computation, at 35
" year's purchase. The ashes made from this peat did
" not prove very good: they cost 1d. per bushel to dig
" and burn, and sold for 2d. when burnt; but most of the
" peat was used for fuel, particularly in brick-kilns and
" hot-houses *."

Woollen Rags.—Mr. FORSTER, at Royston, has a very
high opinion of this manure, especially on chalk for wheat.
He lays on 8 cwt. at 8s. per cwt.

Sticklebacks have been carried into the northern borders
of the county, and used with great success.

Hair.—Mr. CHAPMAN, of Hitchin, tried tanners'
hair on one-third of a small field, malt-dust on another
third, and lime between the two: the hair proved much
the best manure; the malt-dust the next; and the lime
much the worst.

Dung.—At St. Albans, Hatfield, &c. many poor persons employ themselves in picking up dung on the turn-
pike-roads, which they sell to the farmers at 2d. a bushel.
Mr. CLARKE, of Sandridgebury, buys large quantities,
spreading 180 bushels per acre for turnips.

Mr. CHAPMAN, of Hitchin, has observed, that, about
Baldock, they carry out their dung in a remarkably long
state, without rotting, and yet they get as good turnips as
any where.

Mr. ROBERTS, of King's Walden, would always, on
every account, carry stable-dung long and fresh to the

* MS. Annot.

land,

land, but thinks that farm-yard manure should be turned up once, yet not kept too long.

Of the ploughing Dung in.—Mr. DEERMAN, of Astwick, remarked that some farmers leave their dung spread without ploughing, for some time ; arguing, that the rains, when they come, will wash in the salts, and that the sun exhales only water : that his own opinion was very different, and his practice, to turn it in as soon as possible. He is certainly right. For the same reason nearly, he remarked, in shewing me a folded fallow, that turning in the sheep's manure, the effect might be different, as the urine is best ; and that sinking is not, perhaps, so much exhaled as it would be by letting in the sun and air by ploughing *.

Mr. SEDGWICK, of Rickmersworth, lays all his dung on for turnips : he carries it out when he has finished his spring sowing, and then spreads and ploughs it in immediately, but never until the land has been first cleaned from weeds. He is clearly of opinion that long dung is best ; and if it could be carried from the stable, and ploughed in immediately, it would be by far the best.

Manuring in general.—At Sawbridgeworth, on the clays and strong loams, the farms are not large, and few sheep are kept. The cattle are by no means numerous, and chiefly cows for suckling ; nor do the farmers bring manures from London ; little is therefore effected by this branch of management. To make amends for its want, they exert themselves greatly in tillage, fallowing very often. Mr. PARRIS, at the parsonage farm, shewed me his fallows for barley, which had received the dung of his

---

* I think this opinion, relative to land folded by sheep, erroneous. The land should be ploughed, and the dung turned in as soon as possible.—*H.*

yards

yards in June, ploughed in on two-bout ridges ten months before sowing.

At the Hadhams, where the course is fallow for wheat, and then fallow for barley, the best farmers lay on the yard-dung for the barley.

Mr. CASSMAJOR, at North Mims, carrying much hay to London, manures highly. See p. 170.

1. To his turnips he gives six chaldrons of bones, at 10s. 6d. and carriage; or with rabbits'-dung, 20 quarters, at 2s. 8d; but this is now sold as high as 3s. 6d.

2. Barley succeeds turnips, but without any dressing.

3. Clover follows, and has a cart-load an acre of ashes, at 10s.; but this is now sold as high as 20s.

4. Wheat; 40 bushels of soot, at 10d. formerly sold for 7½d. or 8d. per bushel, now 1s.

At Royston, the manures used are oil-dust, woollen rags, rabbits'-dung, malt-dust, and some soot and ashes.

Mr. Doo, of Bygrave, manures to an extraordinary degree, never laying out less than 600l. a year on a farm of 1000 acres, besides his yard-dung and the fold of 1000 large sheep and lambs. For turnips he gives both dung and fold, and 25 to 30 bushels of soot. The sheep also feed always on oil-cake dust; and for the barley which follows, he gives, in addition, never less than two quarters, or forty bushels of soot. For clover, nothing; for the wheat, from 16 to 20 bushels of oil-dust; but less, if the clover was very good. By means of this heavy dressing, he conceives that he gets two loads of wheat and two quarters of barley more per acre, than the same land would yield, were this system not pursued.

Mr. SMITH, at Clothalbury, at the distance of 39 miles from London, used to bring down much soot and

trotters,

trotters, not then keeping many sheep; but he has since left it off, from being convinced that it did not answer so well as dressing by sheep; and he has greatly increased his flock. He now consumes his hay and straw at home, except what he sells to Baldock, from whence he brings dung back.

" Part of Cashiobury-park was dressed in the year
" 1790 with the following compost: about 15,000 cubic
" yards of pond-mud were mixed, when wet, with good
" unslacked chalk-lime; one load, or 40 bushels of lime,
" to about 20 loads of mud, and laid on the poorest soil
" in the park, the staple of which is about four inches on
" chalk. The natural clover sprung up soon afterwards
" in great abundance; and, in 1793, the land so ma-
" nured was (to use the bailiff's words) a perfect honey-
" suckle, and eagerly fed off by the cattle depastured
" thereon. A piece of land by the pond-side, was ma-
" nured with the mud only, and planted with cabbages,
" which are said to have grown to an extraordinary size
" and quality: but the droughts of the summer 1794
" had completely burnt up the honeysuckle; and about
" the middle of August, in that year, Cashiobury, and
" the other Hertfordshire parks, were as grey as bad-
" gers*."

" Messrs. DOWBIGGIN and HAYNES are two very
" successful farmers (tenants of the Marquis of SALIS-
" BURY), and, by means of London manures, render a
" poor pebbly gravel productive †."

A Comparison.—The Writer of this Report, when he lived in Hertfordshire, made the following comparative experiment.

* First Report. + J. HUTCHINSON.

Propor-

Proportions per acre of the manure and the crops of potatoes on a poor gravelly loam.

		Crop.
No.		Bushels.
1.	No manure, - - - -	120
2.	Night-soil, 10 waggon-loads, each 96 bushels,	600
3.	Ditto, 6 loads, - - -	650
4.	Ditto, 2 ditto, - - -	500
5.	Bones, 10 ditto, - - -	650
6.	Ditto, 6 ditto, - - -	640
7.	Ditto, 2 ditto, - - -	560
8.	Hog-dung, 60 one-horse cart-loads, -	480
9.	Ditto, 30 ditto, - - -	480
10.	Yard-compost, 60 ditto, - -	300
11.	Ditto, 120 ditto, - - -	480
12.	Ditto, 30 ditto, - - -	140

In the April following, he planted them again with potatoes.

1.	- - - -	140
2.	- - - -	640
3.	- - - -	500
4.	- - - -	300
5.	- - - -	640
6.	- - - -	560
7.	- - - -	240
8.	- - - -	300
9.	- - - -	160
10.	- - - -	240
11.	- - - -	300
12.	- - - -	140

The principal feature of the trial is the vast effect of bones and night-soil.

HERTS.]   SECT.

SECT. IV.—IRRIGATION.

THE county affords great opportunities for this important work; but it abounds also with so many mills, as to impede it greatly. Some traces of the practice are, however, found, which demand attention.

Mr. WHITTINGTON, at Broadwater, waters a meadow of eight acres by the wash of uplands after rain: it has no other manure, and yields two loads an acre, which, for the soil, is a great improvement. But he observed, that the benefit of irrigation is not so great, as the *quantity* of produce seems to indicate; for he once sent Mr. BENTFIELD some bullocks to eat off a great after-grass in his watered-meadows: the beasts were there some months, but were not improved in the smallest degree.

Mr. BENTFIELD procured a man from the west of England, who watered 40 or 50 acres at Watton-wood Hall. I examined them, but found the works and meadows in the greatest state of neglect, over-run with flags and rushes; but from the direction of the carrier-trenches which I saw, and from the very insufficient drains for taking off the water rapidly, as it ought to be, it appears that these works were ill-planned, and as badly executed. The opportunity for irrigation is great, and may be applied to very considerable profit. The levels, however, should be taken much higher up the stream; for I conceive that some gravelly arable fields might be converted to meadow, if the division of the estate in the sale, has not rendered it at present impossible.

Mr. WANGFORD's father, by leave of the miller, floated a meadow at Bushy, but nothing is done at present.

At Rickmersworth, Mr. SALTER has a watered-meadow on broad ridges, the carriers in the centres, and the drains

in

in the furrows : he was then mowing it a second time, but the crop was not large; apparently the drains are not deep enough, for the herbage is too coarse. But I was afterwards informed by Mr. SEDGWICK, that this meadow is, in general, very productive, and yielded a great crop this year, and is considered as very well-managed. The same intelligent gentleman informs me, that from Cashiobury-bridge to Rickmersworth, and from thence to Uxbridge, there are many watered-meadows, which let from 30s. to 50s. an acre : they are never fed in the spring with ewes and lambs, but generally mown twice ; the first crop gives from one and a half to two loads of hay ; the second a load. The after-grass is fed with cows and heifers ; the meadows are then kept as dry as possible : the farmers begin to water them at Christmas, by which time they are well drained, ready for receiving the water ; of which the most muddy is esteemed to be the best.

Three shillings and sixpence per acre are given for draining and floating. These meadows are all so laid, that the water may run quickly : without watering, they would not let for more than 20s. an acre. There are some also in the parish of King's Langley.

" The watering of the meadows near Rickmersworth, has
" been considered of such consequence by the owners and
" occupiers thereof, that they were long the subject of
" expensive law-suits with an opulent miller at Badg-
" worth, who deeming himself, and those under whom
" he claimed, kings of the waters, broke down the dams,
" sluices, &c. erected for the purpose of flooding, both
" above and below his mill; and when the question
" of right was first tried, he was even so lucky as to get
" a verdict in his favour ; but, about the year 1790, a
" jury was found who differed widely in opinion with
                                                    " their

" their predecessors in office; and his Majesty of Badg-
" worth-mill has since suffered his neighbours to flood
" their meadows without interruption.

" The many streams intersecting this county in every
" direction, and mentioned in the general description
" thereof, may undoubtedly be applied to great advantage
" in watering the meadows and low grounds contiguous
" thereto, if directed with judgment; but while the ques-
" tion of the rights of mill-owners thereon remains in its
" present undetermined state, few occupiers of such lands,
" if they had every other encouragement, will be found
" hardy enough to risk the expense and uncertainty of
" law-suits*."

Although we find it stated in the First Report, that the
water, wherewith meadows are flooded, should be thick,
it is not necessary; for the benefit of flooding is never so
perceptible as in hot dry weather, after cutting the first
crop of hay. When the water is limpid, it is supposed at
that time to carry valuable particles of oil, &c. This was
peculiarly the opinion of Mr. BAKEWELL, of Dishley,
who projected and effected the flowing of land in as capital a manner as any where in England. In fact, it would
be absurd to depend much on the benefit of the sediment
of thick water; where it happens, by some impediment,
to be accumulated, it makes a great appearance, but
where regularly diffused, it is almost imperceptible.

J. HUTCHINSON has mentioned above, his own improvements by flooding. There was a great deal flooded
in the course of the Lea from London to Hatfield; the
people who did the work lived at Whithamsted, and had
5s. per acre for their trouble.

The contests between millers and occupiers of land,

* First Report.

are

are perpetual and universal all over the kingdom. It would be well worthy the attention of the Board, to obtain an equitable decision of the points contested, or likely to be contested : at present, the *fashion* of law is favourable to millers, and unfavourable to flooding, although the latter is considerably more beneficial to society ; for almost any water-mill is capable of flowing, by means of a level taken from its head, more land than would pay the rent of the mill ; and without losing many days' grinding in the year. Mr. BAKEWELL, of Dishley, took a lease of Dishley-mill, which enabled him to improve his land more in its annual value than twice the rent of the mill; but such improvement by no means rendered the mill useless. J. HUTCHINSON made a similar offer to Lord SALISBURY, for an old paper-mill at Hatfield, but it was refused ; he then availed himself of an old prescriptive right of taking water without consent, but it was scarcely sufficient; notwithstanding which, he effected the improvement before-mentioned. Mr. MAWE afterwards took the Salisbury-Arms inn, and with it the demesne-lands which J. HUTCHINSON sold to Lord SALISBURY at Woodhall : he neglected the flowing the meadows, and they became very bad : he has since left the place.

CHAP. XIII.

OF LIVE STOCK.

———

THIS subject, which, in so many counties, from the modern improvements made in it, has so greatly occupied the public attention, and claimed the first consideration from the Reporters, is, perhaps, as barren a one in Hertfordshire as any that can be named. It is merely an arable country ; and the quantity of clover-hay carried to London is so great, and forms so profitable a husbandry, that live stock must be a very inferior object. I did not neglect to make inquiries, and the reader will find some particulars, which merit his attention.

———

SECT. I.——CATTLE.

HERTFORDSHIRE having no breed of its own, the cattle kept in it are of various sorts.

At Sawbridgeworth few are kept, except some Welsh cows for suckling. Mr. PARRIS, at the parsonage-farm, has a malting-office, and applies the *combs*, mixed with barley-meal and cut chaff, to fatten bullocks.

Welsh heifers are Mr. BYDE's chief stock ; he thinks them best adapted to his land : they are bought in at Harlow fair, on the 28th of November ; but he never gives more than 5l. for them : larger heifers have sold at 7l.

Mr. GREG, at West-mill, keeps Suffolk cows : he milks twelve, and finds them to answer fully every expectation.

peﬆation. He procured also twenty-four Suffolk steers, three years old, very good beasts, eight of which he works.

The Rev. Mr. KEATE, at Hatfield, has Suffolk cows, of which he approves highly : one this year fattened her own calf, to the value of 8l. 8s. in eleven weeks; it weighed 20 stone; and to the last, the calf did not suck all her milk.

The Marchioness of SALISBURY keeps a great variety of cattle : Suffolks are found to be the best of all for milk, and the next best are the Welsh. Devons, of which she has some very good, are the best for work and fatting. Her Ladyship has buffaloes, both of the whole and of the half breed, crossed with Scotch and Devon, for veal and beef of a fine quality ; she has also Scotch, Yorkshire, and other cattle. Above 50 cows are kept of all breeds.

Mr. MARSH, at Hatfield, has some poor wet pastures on a *mother*-stone * bottom, which are very apt to give cattle unaccustomed to feed on them, the red water ; but as he has improved some of these fields by draining and manuring, this effeﬆ ceases, as to those fields so improved.

Lady MELBOURNE has Devon, Hereford, and Suffolk cows ; the last, as the bailiff informed me, are the best milkers, and the most profitable : the Devons, on the Brocket land, are better than the Herefords.

Mr. BAKER, at Bayfordbury, has Welsh cattle, bought in at Michaelmas at 7l. to 9l. per head ; they are turned to straw in winter, well fed in summer, and sold at 15l. or 16l. : some are put to turnips and hay, and now and then a good one to oil-cake.

Sir JOHN SEBRIGHT, at Beachwood, has Suffolk cows, and some long and short horned ones, and is convinced that the Suffolks are better than any other which he has tried.

_____
* A vitriolic concretion of blue pebbles.

In

In stall-feeding beasts, Mr. CHAPMAN, of Hitchin, has remarked the advantage of changing the food, for instance, clover-hay for meadow-hay, and meadow for clover-hay; and he is clear in this point.

Mr. HALE, of King's Walden, has Devonshires only, and approves of them much.

Lord GRIMSTON has the spotted polled breed from Mr. MUNDY of Derbyshire, and approves of the sort greatly.

About Rickmersworth they generally find, and Mr. SEDGWICK also agrees in it, that no cows bought in, answer like those bred on the spot, which are commonly the long-horned: the difference is very great; they are used chiefly for suckling calves; and the Rickmersworth meadows, the soil of which is a peat, whether watered or not, are famous for white veal.

Mr. PARKER, of Munden, has had Devonshires and Herefords, which are very good breeds for both work and fatting; but neither of them at all proper to stock a dairy; six quarts of milk at a meal is a common produce of a Devonshire: and the Herefords are much on a par. Coarse Herefords are more common than Devons; but if bred as they ought to be, the Herefords are equal in flesh and work, with the advantage of coming to a much greater weight and value. The short-horned cows are far better milkers; and Alderneys better than any; but the bull calves of that breed are a great loss.

Mr. THELLUSON, of Munden, has had Devon cows hitherto; but finding them bad milkers, is about to change them for short-horns.

The Earl of ESSEX has short-horned Yorkshire cows at present; but Devons and Suffolks were at Cashiobury, and the latter, in Mr. BISHOP's opinion, much better than the short-horned. Suffolks, he thinks, preferable to

any,

any, except the best of the Welsh, which, when well
selected, are an excellent breed.

Mr. CALVERT, at Albury, when oil-cake was much
cheaper than at present, found it the most advantageous
and profitable food that he could give his cows: three
cakes a day, with eight or ten pounds of hay, or four
cakes and good straw, were the usual allowance; two were
given to cows in calf and to growing heifers: he practised this till cake advanced beyond 9l. a thousand. How
far it may answer at much higher prices, hay and butter
having both greatly advanced, careful experiments will
alone ascertain, which he himself should have made; but
Swedish turnips being introduced, and answering uncommonly well, he lost the inducement to go on with the
other food. Cake gave very good butter; and, at 6l. or 7l.
a thousand, was the cheapest food that could be given.

Mr. DOO, of Bygrave, prefers small to large cattle,
thinking that they meet in general a readier sale and a better price, especially in the country: yet he admits, that
cattle do not eat in proportion to their weight; and in-
stanced a Welsh beast that he fed with cake, by the side
of a large Hereford ox, the latter of 160 stone, and the
Welsh not 90. The Hereford ate six cakes a day, and
the other five. I saw the Hereford, which is a fine beast.
Experiments are much wanting, that shall accurately ascertain the value of cake in feeding.

SECT. II.—SHEEP.

Mr. PLUMMER, at Gilston, keeps 200 Wiltshire
ewes, which he folds with their lambs till November, and
by close feeding his lawn, renders this little flock one of
the

the means of adding profitably to the beauty of his place. He sells his wether lambs from 15s. to 20s. I recommended South Downs in preference ; but he said that it had been found necessary, by some persons who had tried them on a clay soil, to change them every three years, which, at such a distance from Sussex, and at such prices as those for which this breed sold, would form a troublesome and expensive system. Query the fact ? as it is not found to be the case with Wiltshire sheep.

Mr. BYDE, of Ware-Park, has long been in the practice of keeping Wiltshire ewes, and has had so good a breed of them, as to sell rams at eight and ten guineas each. He once sold four three-year old wethers for 32 guineas. He has now changed his system, and I found 420 South Down wether lambs just arrived from Linfield fair, in Sussex. He proposes to buy 400 wether lambs of that breed in August, and to put them on grass after the head flock, and fold them till near Christmas ; then to put them to turnips, and in the spring on reserved grass on poor land, to fold them again till Michaelmas, and then to turnip them for the butcher ; so as to clear all off before they shall be two years old. He expects to buy at 21s. and to sell at 45s. The fleece weighs three pounds and a half each, and the tod of 28lb. sells for 47s. These sheep will fold one acre and a half a week, or 45 acres in 30 weeks, and to the value of 70l.

Mr. JONES, of Little Hadham, has South Downs, which he prefers to Wiltshires : the latter have the goggles often, but the South Downs never. The long-legged Wiltshire, however, in his opinion, suffer less in folding on wet land.

Mr. GREG, of Westmill, has 360 of a mixed breed, between Cotteswold and the new Leicester. I examined, and found them of a large frame ; shearlings come to 24lb.

a quarter,

a quarter, and some to more: he sells fat lambs in June
at 36s. to 42s. The fleece weighs six pounds; so that
the account may be profitable. But I cannot approve of
folding these, or any other sheep, in such a heavy country.
The benefit of the fold is not the question, for that is un-
disputed: but do not the sheep suffer more than to the value
of the fold? And how many might be kept if not folded?

He has lately imported a parcel from Sherwood Forest;
they leaped the fold; broke through the hedges, and fo-
raged where they chose. It is a breed not calculated for
the country.

Mr. Rook, of Bengeo, has found, on comparison,
that oil-cake at 18l. 18s. per ton, was a cheaper food for
sheep than clover-hay at 7l. per load. The experiment
was a considerable one, for they ate 30l. a week in cake.

The Rev. Mr. Keate, at Hatfield, feeds Wiltshire
sheep on oil-cake: while at turnips, he allows them two
pounds a day; and is confident that it answers, even at
20l. a thousand: the manuring, which the land thus receives, is very valuable.

The Marchioness of Salisbury keeps a breed between the Cotteswold and Leicester; and some that
have a little West Indian blood, for fineness of bone; but
this breed having an aptitude to be lean, little of it is preserved. Some of the sheep here have good carcasses; but
an unquestionable improvement would result from a total
change of this breed for a South Down flock. The remark, however, does not extend to the Park system, of
buying in Welsh ewes at 7s. or 8s. and selling lamb and
ewe from 20s. to 30s.: this is profitable.

I had some conversation with Mr. Stephenson on
folding: he is decidedly against the practice; and remarked, that the farmers know not what they lose by it:
the ewe and lamb are both greatly injured; and certainly
a less

a less flock is kept by means of this practice, than might be without it.

Mr. CASSMAJOR has South Down sheep, and his bailiff, ROBERTS, who has great experience, approves of them. The result of the comparison here seems to be, that South Down do better on grass-land than Wiltshires, and will in that case thrive more, and better support the hardships of short food; but on arable land, with plenty of turnips, clover rye, tares, &c. in ample provision, the Wiltshires are more profitable than South Downs. The Wiltshires are large sheep, and consequently require to be well kept.

At Bayfordbury, Mr. BAKER finds that a wether flock suits the soil, either gravel on mother-stone, or strong and wet, better than breeding. He buys Wiltshires at two years old, from 25s. to 37s. each, and sells them after a year's feeding, from 40s. to 80s.; the fleece weighs four pounds: a tod of 28lb. sells for 35s. Sometimes he buys lambs, and sells them at three years old: he buys in at 20s. or 21s. and sells out from 40s. to 80s. The bailiff, Mr. ROBERTS, assured me that they are constantly folded, the drive to the fold being short; but the attempt to fold fatting sheep is not common.

Mr. YOUNG, at Hurral, has two flocks, a breeding and a wether flock: the sort should depend on the feeding; when that is ample, Wiltshires will pay best: but he approves greatly of South Downs, and especially when they are to undergo any hardships. While his fat wethers eat turnips they have oil-cake in troughs, half a cake a day to each sheep; and this, let the price of cake be what it may. It answers well, and gives great barley crops.

Mr. CLARKE, of Sandridgebury, keeps a breeding flock of Wiltshires. They take the ram in August, are put to turnips as soon as they lamb, and he sells the lambs fat from

from Easter to Michaelmas, at 39s. or 40s. on an average: he draws off his old ewes for turnips early, and sells them from 30s. to 40s.

At Mr. RAPER's, near Berkhamsted, I saw some good South Downs, but he was absent, and nobody was there, of whom I could make inquiries.

Col. DORRIEN was also absent, but his bailiff informed me, that the Colonel buys 100 South Down wethers every year: he has had six new Leicester ewes for an experiment, and three of them proved barren; the other three, however, produced five lambs.

Every farmer about Berkhamsted has his fold, and many of the sheep are fed on commons: the sheep are Wiltshires, and some Berkshire sheep without horns; but the former are the most approved: the Duke of BRIDGE-WATER, at Ashridge, has a flock of a mixed breed, almost of South Down blood, raised by crossing 400 Norfolks, procured from the Duke of GRAFTON, gradually with South Down rams, till they are become almost whole blooded South Downs: he keeps 1000 in all. They have not been free from the goggles.

Sir JOHN SEBRIGHT has 300 half and whole-bred South Downs: the cross is with the new Leicester: he sells no lambs.

About Beachwood, &c. the general breed is from Wiltshire, and the flocks are, in general, wethers: they buy in lambs, or shearlings, and keep the latter one year to fold, and half a year to fat. They sell them in the spring; buy them in from 30s. to 40s. and sell them from 45s. to 60s. The fleece is worth 3s. and the fold 40s. an acre. 100 will fold more than ten acres in the season. The fold is first set about the end of April, and taken away a month after Michaelmas.

Mr. PARKYN, of Dunstable, has 500 South Downs: he

he has tried new Leicesters, but esteems South Downs as the most profitable.

Mr. HALE, of King's Walden, has had South Downs five or six years, and he thinks nothing beats them, where there is much grass; but on artificial grass and turnips, without a breadth of natural grass, they will not do like the Wiltshires; for which reason Mr. ROBERTS, on his own farm, keeps Wiltshire ewes, and crosses them with South Down rams; so that they lamb in March. When put to grass, they are folded, and some lambs are sold at 34s. in the beginning of harvest; some twins at 31s. 6d. and the best are kept. He approves so much of them, that he intends to continue them. I viewed Mr. HALE's flock with pleasure: they form a capital one, and the wool is remarkably fine: they are the best flock of South Downs which I have seen in Hertfordshire. He was absent himself, or I should have had a more particular detail.

Lord GRIMSTON has only South Down wethers at Gorhambury, which he buys annually at Linfield fair, in Sussex: he has had the breed here 23 years. At first he used to buy them at 8s. or 9s. a-head: this year he bought 220 at 20s.; last year at 15s. 6d.; the year before that, at 17s. He folds them constantly till November, when he begins to fatten, and sells them in the spring, when three years old, from 3l. to 4l. 10s. per head, and some, last year, were sold at 5l. Those bought at 15s. 6d. were sold at 3l. 10s. He very rarely gives hay. They have been remarkably healthy, and the losses were very trifling. Some of his Lordship's tenants also have them, and they are coming generally into repute. It is, however, thought, that the Wiltshires fatten better on turnips: a tod of South Down wool, weighing 28lb. is sold for 44s.; of Wiltshire, for 35s.

Mr.

Mr. KINGSMAN has had South Downs four years; a breeding stock; and brings his rams from Sussex. He finds them a very beneficial stock, and very hardy. He sells off all his lambs fat, excepting only the ewe lambs, reserved for keeping up the flock. These lambs are sold fat in the course of the summer: the ewes have never any hay in winter, and are put on turnips only as they lamb.

The reserve consists of 50 lambs, which are kept through the winter on grass, with either hay or turnips. The lambs sold have neither cake nor corn, yet are sold, in the course of the summer, for 29s. and 30s. to 34s. The prices of this year are as under:

1801	June 3,	-	-	-	15,	at	29s.
	— 13,	-	-		10,	—	30s.
	July 2,	-	-		10,	—	29s.
	Sept. 15,	-		-	10,	—	34s.
1800	Aug. 4,	-		-	4,	—	27s.
	Sept. 13,	-	-		10,	—	26s.
	Oct. 18,	-	-		12,	—	25s.
	————	-		-	6,	—	23s.
	————	-	-		5,	—	22s.

Lord CLARENDON has had Cotteswold wethers, which fat well; Ryeland and South Down ewes, crossed by new Leicester rams, which answer very well at the first trial: he has also Norfolk wethers for the table. He feeds ewes and lambs with turnips and oil-cake, until about the middle of May; the cake is ground, and a little given twice a day with chaff. Ewes and lambs all go off fat, and it answers greatly in forwarding the lambs; all of which are sold off by the end of June.

He has bought in Ryeland ewes for 25s. per head, in September, and put new Leicester rams to them: all produced

duced twins; and the best lambs sold at 30s.; the rest at 24s. The ewes weighed 7 stone of 8 lb.: they fattened quickly, were easily fed, and were very quiet.

His troughs for giving cake are very well contrived, with a roof sloping over them, covering the sheep's head and neck while feeding; a precaution found necessary, as rain spoils the cake.

Mr. NEWMAN, at Hatley, keeps new Leicesters, and finds them hardier than Wiltshires, and much more profitable, as they keep themselves fat, while the other breed will be lean. He buys wether and ewe lambs every year at Northampton fair.

At Rickmersworth, Mr. SEDGWICK, and several other considerable farmers, are largely in the suckling of house-lambs: they breed entirely Dorsetshire or Wiltshire ewes : 100 old stock, and 50 bought at Michaelmas, will produce 200 lambs, exclusive of double lambs, on an average of years : the 100 old produce 100 lambs at Christmas, the 50 new produce 50 lambs in October, and 50 more in July; all are sold within the year. The farmers choose their rams short-legged; and white barbs in the mouth and eyes, as they choose a calf, with a white nose and a white hoof. They sell sheep as high as 4l. and 4l. 4s. but 30s. the average price of 200. Mr. SEDGWICK conceives that a trussed load of straw will make a wag-gon-load of dung. In the winter, they feed their ewes and lambs with grains and malt-dust.

Mr. PARKER, of Munden, has had new Leicesters about three years, and has since bred from them; he approves of them much for a disposition to fat, and for hardiness; but if they are at all *fine*, they demand attention when they lamb. He has also a high opinion of South Downs, but is inclined to prefer the new Leicesters.

ters. If allowed to be too fat, they will run barren, and the rams, if bred too fine, may be good for nothing : but Mr. PARKER conceives, that by proper attention, these evils may be easily prevented. The fleece weighs from five to six pounds. Mr. PARKER can sell them fat when shearlings ; but they are sold more usually when twice shorn. He never folds any sheep, nor can reconcile it to any principles of common sense, to take from one field in order to enrich another: if any folding can be admitted, it is in the heat of the day, when they fold themselves in ditches, and would do it in a covered fold, were there one in the field ; but if the sheep are fed on a common, this reasoning does not apply.

Mr. THELLUSON, of Munden, has a flock of South Downs ; a breed of which he much approves.

The Earl of ESSEX keeps a large number of South Down wethers, bought in every year: this season full-mouthed wethers cost 47s. 6d. each, and wether lambs 24s. 6d.

Between thirty and forty years since, Mr. CALVERT, of Albury, had Lincoln sheep, but sold them, from conviction that they did not answer: he was then for about twenty years in the Wiltshire breed ; and, lastly, he changed these for the South Downs, which he has had for the last seven or eight years, and prefers them to all. He has no other than Lord PELHAM's breed, both rams and ewes, and considers the more modern attempts to raise a *finer* race, as likely to prove mischievous : he will not have any thing to do with them. His six-toothed wethers weigh eleven stone and a half. He finds the breed extremely healthy ; they very rarely die ; and are subject to much fewer distempers than the Wiltshires.

HERTS.]   About

About Barkway, South Downs are not yet introduced, and Mr. HILL, of Whittle, gave it as his decided opinion, that, *feed and work* Wiltshires and South Downs *together, and in the same manner,* and the former will prove to be the most profitable ; the latter are much injured by the dirt, as they are too short in hair and legs: it was tried at Kimpton Hoo, and such was the result. He has sold Wiltshire wethers thrice shorn, at 7l. 14s. each.

Mr. Doo, of Bygrave, keeps Wiltshire ewes, which he crosses every year by new Leicester rams ; but goes no farther than the first cross. These answer greatly, whether the sale be of fat lambs or shearlings. He does not approve of South Downs, on account of their inferior weight.

Mr. SMITH, of Clothalbury, has changed Wiltshires for South Downs. At the last sheep-shearing at Woburn he exhibited a specimen of each : at that meeting I heard it remarked, that without doubt he had picked the worst Wiltshires and the best South Downs. Mr. SMITH knew nothing of my coming, and therefore I found his flock without any selection : he has about 400 in all, some few of them Wiltshires ; they are *fed and worked together,* and folded on wet land, in a field, where I saw hollow drainers at work on a fallow for wheat: the South Downs are in exceeding good order, and the Wiltshires are very inferior.

Fold.—In the clay district of the county, Mr. BYDE remarks that sheep have been too much lessened. Of all the common manures, he considers the fold as the best ; and he has observed in many farms the general appearance of the crops decline, as the number of sheep kept has lessened.

At the Hadhams, every man folds the sheep which he

keeps :

keeps: a little farmer will even set four hurdles, if he has not sheep for more.

Good as the manure of the fold is, Mr. CHAPMAN has found by trial in the same field, for turnips, that yard-dung was much better than both fold and malt-dust together.

Mr. ROBERTS, of King's Walden, thinks nothing is equal to the fold: he never reckoned it worth less than 40s. per acre, corn being cheap; but of late much more: he folds two poles of ground with 20 sheep.

Mr. SEDGWICK, of Rickmersworth, is clearly in favour of folding on all farms.

The Earl of CLARENDON, at the Grove, folds in the yard, from the end of October to the end of March. I viewed the fold with much pleasure; it contains good room for 300, the number kept in it: an open shed surrounds it, except on one side, where a barn is the fence; the outside of the shed is formed of wattled hurdle-work, without straw, or other materials, for coolness, lest a greater closeness should make the yard too hot: it is all kept well littered with stubble, and yields, from 300 sheep, 80 large cart-loads of manure. This system agrees perfectly well with the sheep, and keeps them more healthy than when they were left in the fields in the common manner. His Lordship has another yard for lambing, which has also a shed.

The most interesting feature of these minutes, is the comparison of the Wiltshire and South Down breeds. Amongst very practical and reasonable men, the notion of the former doing best on turnips, and the latter on grass, has gained such ground, that I can scarcely conceive it to be a mere prejudice; and I ought to remark, that I have in other counties, and on various occasions, met with so

many

many instances of Wiltshire wethers paying greatly for turnips, that I am inclined to think there is much truth in the Hertfordshire notion. Let me combine it with another well-known fact, which is, that the Norfolk breed also pay remarkably well while fatting on turnips, I take these two breeds to be, generally speaking, the worst in the kingdom: it is, therefore, somewhat remarkable, that they should agree in this point of merit. It is sufficiently evident, that accurate experiments (by no means easy to make) are much wanted, clearly to ascertain such facts ; which certainly ought to be ascertained more satisfactorily than any general ideas or remarks, or general experience can effect. In the very interesting experiments made by the Duke of BEDFORD, registered in *Annals of Agriculture*, vol. xxiii. p. 456, and vol. xxvi. p. 412, nothing of this sort occurs in favour of the Wiltshires.

SECT. III.—HORSES.

THIS subject is interesting in husbandry, chiefly in relation to the means of lessening the number kept; and of feeding those that must be kept, in the cheapest manner.

Sir JOHN SEBRIGHT has both Suffolks and blacks, and is convinced from much experience, that the former have a decided superiority.

Mr. SEDGWICK remarks, that the staggers and yellows are generally most heard of in September, &c. ; and he attributes it to the food not being changed. He is convinced that green food is not wholesome after August : he always puts them to hay and corn about the 1st of September,

ber, instead of soiling on the second growth of clover, at a season when it is watery. He allows seven bushels of oats a week to four horses, but gives none for three months; a load of hay lasts four horses three weeks.

Four horses from Hatfield to London, 20 miles, draw three loads of straw; and two and two loads and a half of hay. Three horses draw one load of hay in a cart, if they are to bring a heavy load of manure back. Four horses draw from St. Albans from one load and a half to two loads of hay twice a week.

From Watford, and the vicinity, four horses draw a load and a half of hay three times a week.

About Beachwood, and indeed generally every where, four horses are allowed to 100 acres of arable land : four horses take one load and a half of hay to London, 30 miles, and bring 160 bushels of soot back; it employs three days, and they can do it twice a week ; but that is hard work. They commonly give their horses a peck of oats a day, but when they soil them, only the half.

About Gorhambury, the expense per horse is estimated at 20l. on an average, in food and shoeing.

To 80 acres of arable here, four horses are allowed by one man; the same number by another to 100 acres ; and to 120 acres, six horses.

At Rickmersworth, they allow four horses for 100 acres, and six for 130.

Mr. KING, of Barkway, in a six-inch wheeled waggon, drawn by six horses, carries 40 quarters of porter malt*, a four-bushel sack of which weighs from 135 pounds to 140 pounds, 160 miles a week in constant work. This amounts to 320 bushels, or 53 bushels and a

* Porter malt weighs five pounds a bushel lighter than pale malt.

small

small fraction, per horse, which, at 34 pounds per bushel, makes each horse's load 1802 pounds : this is very great and uncommon loading for 26 miles a day. The same horses draw also 30 quarters of barley, at 15 stone a comb, or 52 pounds a bushel, from Cambridge to Ware, and load back with oil-cake, 2500 cakes, at two pounds and a half each ; each horse draws of barley 2080 pounds, and of cake 1041 pounds. They are, as may be supposed, very capital horses, bought in Suffolk ; but their feeding is as capital, for the six horses have five bushels of oats a week, and 9 cwt. of hay.

Soiling.—At Sawbridgeworth, I observed a very fine crop of clover mowing regularly, for soiling the teams in the stable.

Mr. BYDE, of Ware-Park, feeds his teams thus all summer : he gives them tares as long as they last, and then clover ; he observes, that some caution should be used in filling the racks, for servants are apt to give too much at once, so that he has from that cause nearly lost several horses by the gripes : he uses castor-oil in half pint doses till it operates, as the remedy for them.

Soiling is common every where : about Berkhamsted the best farmers never turn out ; they begin with winter tares, which are ashed in February at the rate of eight sacks an acre ; then clover is given, then spring tares ; and afterwards the second crop of clover, to Michaelmas.

Around Beachwood, soiling lasts about three months.

About Hitchin, they soil much, but chiefly on tares : the same is practised at King's Walden ; and on clover also.

About Rickmersworth, four acres of tares are allowed to eight horses, and then as much clover.

To

To multiply notes on a practice so very general in the county, would be useless, as the mere repetitions must be numerous: it is sufficient to observe, that I found it general in every part of the county; and it certainly forms a feature of uncommon merit in the husbandry of Hertfordshire: I know not any district where it is equally general. The farmers are clearly decided in the great advantages attending the practice; not only in supporting the teams in the cheapest manner, but also in raising large quantities of very valuable manure.

SECT. IV.——HORSES AND OXEN COMPARED.

THE use of oxen in husbandry is not a common practice in any part of the county; in general, it is confined to gentlemen farmers, the case in many parts of the kingdom; and a circumstance which tends to throw much doubt upon the question of comparison in ascertaining which is the more beneficial team.

Mr. GREG works Suffolk oxen in harness; and finds them to be remarkably handy and docile; he broke them in with scarcely any trouble, and four plough his stiff soil without difficulty. Before he had these, he worked longhorned beasts, but the Suffolk he finds much better. Three will plough land in tilth.

Mr. WHITTINGTON works four teams, 16 oxen, and has been six or seven years in the practice: he uses Hereford and Sussex beasts, and approves of both: four in a plough will do three roods a day, and four horses an acre: he has no doubt of their answering greatly. He works them

on

on straw and turnips, but never on straw only * ; and never
gives them either oats or bran, but oil-cake, which, as he
thinks, answers greatly for them ; a cake and a half a day
with straw, being better than hay; yet cakes are cheaper,
and keep the beasts in better condition. In barley sowing,
the oxen work well, thus fed on cake and barley straw. He
works them on grass ; but they do better on tares. He
uses them from four years old to eight, and they are the
better for fatting †. He has shod some, but thinks, when
the land is not excessively stony, they do better without.
Mr. BECKFORD, at Offley, never shoes his oxen, and
finds no inconvenience from it.

The Marchioness of SALISBURY works Devonshire
oxen, and finds them very beneficial : her bailiff, Mr.

---

* I work oxen, generally, two at a time, for half a day, in a plough with
one man, and three in length or abreast, to break up my wheat or oat stubbles
in winter, after wheat sowing. I work them, as Mr. WHITTINGTON, on
turnips and straw, in the winter ; on straw, and half a peck per day of oat and
barley-meal, mixed in equal proportions, in the spring ; and on grass in the
summer : when their grass is short, or bad, as the case has been sometimes, I
then soil them with clover, mown 24 hours before it is given them. I work two
with one man, and relieve them at noon with the other pair. They will plough
three-quarters of an acre per day in breaking up land ; but I prefer using three
for that purpose, as they will do an acre, and the work is less hard for the
oxen. I have now 20, which I call five teams, and propose to increase them
to 24, or six in the spring, summer, and autumn, and for winter will give four
teams, of six in a team, to break up the wheat and oat stubbles in fallowing the
land. Some of my oxen, in certain fields belonging to me, and in second or third
ploughings, will plough an acre. There is one great advantage in ploughing
with oxen, to which use alone I apply them—they cannot be hurried on like
horses, and the land half ploughed. I could say a great deal more on the subject ; but a note ought not to swell into a dissertation.

I have had fifteen years experience of them ; they will, when wanted,
cart well.—H.

† I now work my oxen from three years and a half old to seven and a half ;
but have worked them to the age of eleven and twelve : I now breed and
rear them from calves. They may be kept too long.—H.

STEPHEN-

STEPHENSON, who is a very observing intelligent man, has no doubt of the utility of working oxen.

Mr. CASSMAJOR, of North Mims, has had twelve years experience of oxen, and therefore I was desirous of conversing with him on the subject, and on the means he took for my information were highly candid and praiseworthy: he is strongly in favour of them; his bailiff, ROBERTS, a sensible, keen, able man, of great experience, is rather adverse to them; he sent for him on that account, in order that no prejudice should influence me, and that I should hear accurately each side of the question. With a master sensible and clear-headed, as well as his man, and both of long experience (for the great losses which Mr. CASSMAJOR had experienced in horses first drove him to the use of oxen), I had every reason to consider myself fortunate: a liberal mind, like that of this gentleman, is ever pleased with a servant in such an office, frankly supporting his own opinion; and the information thus doubly given, and corrected from a cross information, could not fail to be valuable.

Work.—Five oxen form the team for road-work; they draw a cart with a trussed load of hay, or 18 cwt.; and will, if necessary, go twice a week to London, bringing back a load of manure, at the distance of 18 miles. Four horses do the same work *; and will, if necessary, go thrice a week; but it is admitted that the oxen are more proper for home-work than for the road, as they will not go thrice a week, their feet being apt to fail; they throw off their shoes very often. Every ox bought in will not stand this work, not even a fourth part of those purchased; for such

* In a cart, a load; in a waggon, a load and a half, or two loads.

work,

work, it is necessary to buy and try many, and to pick out the best : this is not the case with horses.

Three oxen in a foot-plough do three roods a day ; three horses in a foot plough do an acre : with a wheel-plough four horses do five roods : and four oxen an acre.

It is necessary to observe, that Mr. CASSMAJOR's oxen are of a small size, compared with many ; they are good beasts of the smaller Sussex or Devonshire mould ; they are said to be from Devonshire, but if so, certainly not of the best blood, which is evident from various points: all which I saw were too thick in the leg for that breed, and I did not see one clear thin horn: they are unquestionably of an inferior mould, or this great inferiority to horses would not probably be found in them.

Food.—Four cart-horses eat ten trusses of clover a week, and take besides a truss to London every journey : each horse has also seven pecks of oats a week, and the team takes two pecks to London every journey.

Each ox eats four trusses and a third of hay per week, and have in every journey to London two trusses, but no oats at any time.

The horses, for ten months of the year, are fed in the stable, as stated ; for two months have mown clover in the stable, and no corn for four weeks in harvest.

In regard to shoeing, farrier, and decline of value, we must examine Mr. ROBERTS : he positively asserts that, in Mr. CASSMAJOR's practice, shoeing is against the oxen ; they cost the same as horses, every time 2s. 4d. ; horses 12 times in a year, and oxen 24 upon an average : Mr. CASSMAJOR did not contradict it.

In regard to decline of value, Mr. ROBERTS will admit none in horses, but, on the contrary, in many cases profit, and in all, with tolerable management, a profit on

some

some equal to the decline in others. He buys two-year old colts at 15l. to 26l. and sells them after four, five, or six years work at from 30l. to 40l.; whereas, if the oxen are worked four years, and suffer no loss, it is as much as Mr. CASSMAJOR can do on an average.

In this part of the comparison, there are great difficulties, not easily to be solved, except by recourse to private books, to examine a long series of facts.

Mr. ROBERTS, when he urges the hard work of horses, cannot mean two-year old colts, such as he buys. At three *, he asserts they will stand hard work; but here is a year in which they will *not* stand hard work; and to work a three-year old in such a manner as to place him above oxen, that is, to send him more than twice a week to London, would be little short of insanity. Here, then, Mr. CASSMAJOR has the better of the argument clearly; and it should seem that this circumstance, which is very important, must at least do away all superiority of horses in the point of buying and selling: in my opinion, it goes further, and gives the advantage to the oxen. Making money by horses I admit to be not uncommon, but I know, also, that those who are in the habit of doing it, work them carefully and tenderly.

I must make a remark on the loads drawn by these oxen: a trussed load of hay of 18 cwt. by five oxen, is 403 lb. per ox: one would really think that such a load was given them in ridicule: I may venture to assert, that a good jack-ass, the feeding of which would cost next to nothing, would in a small Irish car that I have, and which was made for that animal, draw such a load: I have had Sussex oxen

---

* Since this was written, Mr. CASSMAJOR informs me by letter, that he does not look for constant work from a colt till he is four years old.

that

that drew four, four and a half, and even five quarters of wheat in single ox-carts ; horses single in Scotland, draw 28 cwt. every day in their common work ; such loads in Hertfordshire, therefore, disgrace the use of oxen.

Some other circumstances relative to Mr. CASSMAJOR's oxen are, that he has tried them in yokes and bows, and is decidedly in favour of harness: it is a point in which he has not the smallest doubt ; and his bailiff concurs entirely in this opinion.

He always shoes them, by casting, which he thinks preferable to doing it in a break : their legs not being tied to any fixture, are not so apt to be strained or bruised ; but it is essential for safety, to do it on an empty stomach, and before they drink.

The course of feeding is on hay only, from the beginning of November to the middle of May, if worked ; if no work, in the straw-yard : in May they are turned to grass, never in the best pastures : but they do much better on dry meat than on green food.

The most profitable system is to work them four years, and then sell, or fat them ; but Mr. CASSMAJOR has worked an ox, and successfully, till twelve years old, and then sold him fat for 35l.

In regard to attendance, it is nearly the same, not of necessity, but through custom.

The prices at which he has bought during twelve years, have been from 12l. to 21l.

Mr. CASSMAJOR's farm contains 200 acres arable, 140 acres of grass mown, and 60 fed ; and his teams consist of ten oxen and four cart-horses.

I asked Mr. ROBERTS whether, if he farmed for himself, he would have any thing to do with oxen ? His an-

swer

swer was, *horses for me :* but recollecting himself, added, *if three teams are kept, I think one should be oxen.*

The conclusion I am much inclined to draw from the whole of this account is, that to render oxen profitable, without breeding, and having an increase in annual value while at work—is to buy none but the largest beasts, that have the full power of the best horses ; to feed them as well as horses ; and to make them do all the work at carting, which they are able to perform ; each should have his cart, and it is the same with horses ; and as to ploughing (except breaking up a fallow for the first time in dry weather, which is never necessary, if the land be ploughed in autumn), a pair of stout oxen is equal to any work, and to an acre a day. Thus managed, I conceive the account would be very different from the preceding.

Mr. ROBERT YOUNG, of Hurral, has worked oxen, and approves of them ; and found Herefords the best of those which he has tried: he has never used Sussex. Four well kept will plough an acre a day, except at breaking up fallows ; but they do not stand well on very flinty land. He has bought oxen at 18l. worked them one summer, and fed them with turnips and oil-cake in the winter, to 40l. Oxen, when turned at night into a very good pasture, do well in the stable on green tares in the day : much depends on feeding them well, for he conceives most of the failures with oxen, to have arisen from the erroneous idea that they need not be highly kept. Four have carried fifteen quarters of malt nineteen miles in the day, the same load as horses ; they returned only an hour or two later ; but they were well fed. In general, the difference between their work and that of horses in ploughing, is one-fifth : four horses do five roods ; four oxen one acre.

The

The Honourable GEORGE VILLIERS, at Aldenham, works Devon oxen in harness, and finds them more profitable than horses.

The Duke of BRIDGEWATER has three teams; and his Grace's opinion (as reported to me by his bailiff) is, that, where there are several teams of horses kept, to have one or two of oxen, as auxiliary teams, is profitable *.

Lord CLARENDON has worked as many as eight; the best breed for quickness and activity are the Devonshires, which will do as much work as horses in carting, but fail at the busy time in spring sowing: horses then are far superior. They feed on grass and hay; and are soiled on tares, on which they do well.

" Bullocks are very improperly said, in the First Report,
" to be fittest for strong heavy lands; for they poach and
" spoil the land, and tire themselves much worse than
" horses: it can only answer to keep them where there is
" plenty of pasture land of moderate value, and where wages
" of men are low; because, by reason of their slowness, a
" great deal of the time of those employed about them
" is lost †."

Mr. LEACH thinks that where four teams are kept, one should be oxen; and every man that keeps a bull, ought to have him broke into a cart for all sorts of jobs. A bull will work more hours than a horse, and wants very little attendance afterwards; and in point of strength, he will draw to the full as much as an ox. When oxen work well, keep them till ten years old, then fat them: all Mr. LEACH's have done remarkably well; one even at thirteen years old. He has often drawn four tons in a waggon six miles with four Devonshire oxen; and has two now which frequently

---

* They should always be kept to the plough.—*H.*
† MS. Annotations, J. HUTCHINSON.

go with a ton and a half of flour to Edgware, ten miles, much up-hill, and bring a load of hay back : these are in harness; they are considerably more profitable in harness than in yokes. The late Earl of Essex had them in yokes, but changed the yokes into harness; as did the Marquis of Abercorn. A single bullock has drawn four tons some small distance on level ground. They plough well, even in flinty land, but often want shoeing : much care is necessary in shoeing, as the oxen are apt to lose their shoes for want of attention.

The following valuable observations, by the Hon. Geo. Villiers, merit the attention of every intelligent reader.

" Dear sir,

" As you have expressed a wish that I should give you " my opinion respecting the comparative use of horses and " oxen, I will venture briefly to state the result of my " own observation ; but with regard to any minute cal-" culation on their food, I must confess that I consider " it an endless point, to watch the distribution of their " provender with a degree of accuracy sufficient to derive " any fair inference from it for permanent practice, as I " am certain that no beasts are fed (taking the chance of " servants) without waste and inattention : for instance, " in travelling the roads near London, no act of roguery " is more frequent than that of the carter disposing of the " hay he takes out, instead of baiting the animals entrusted " to his care.

" It is certainly very possible, and practicable, to " watch the consumption of a given number of animals for " a given time ; but this mode of proceeding would not " meet the common ordinary practice ; and as estimates " given in a loose manner, answer no good purpose, but, " on the contrary, tend to mislead, all I can pretend to

" give

" give you, are only a few general remarks on the sub-
" ject now before us.

" I have found by experience, that business is best con-
" ducted on a farm by a certain number both of bullocks
" *and* horses, especially where there is much road-work
" connected with it.   Six bullocks are about equal to
" four strong cart-horses, in their earning and expense of
" keep; but much will depend, in this comparative view,
" whether the bullocks are in a soil where shoeing will be
" unnecessary, and what may be the relative price of hay
" and oats. I have often heard that bullocks will plough an
" acre of strong land in as short a time as horses : I have
" not found this to be the case ; but though they may re-
" main two hours longer in the field, they do not require
" stable attendance after their work.   They cannot bear
" heat in the summer months equal to horses, and there-
" fore (with me) they enter upon their work at two or
" three o'clock in the morning, by which means they
" nearly complete their business in the cool part of the day.
" However, the point on which I lay my greatest stress,
" on the advantage of bullocks over horses, is on the few
" (comparative) diseases to which the former are subject,
" and which instantly reduce the value of the latter per-
" haps from forty to four guineas.   Spavins, grease, can-
" kers, broken wind, blindness, farcy, mange, are all
" disorders very common among farm horses, not to men-
" tion more frequent injuries than to bullocks, from colds,
" kicks, and bad shoeing : on the other hand, except
" where a bullock appears to have too relaxed and weak
" a habit, I know of no disorder which reduces his real
" value; and it rests with his owner what improvement he
" wishes him to make for the butcher whilst in the yoke.
" I can only say, that from moderate daily work, with
                                                    " one

" one month's rest, I have sent very good bullocks to
" Smithfield market. I am against working them after
" six years old, and they should begin with moderate
" work at two. My system is, to rear about ten or fif-
" teen calves every spring; and, till they come into
" work, they want no extraordinary care or keep; they
" are soon weaned *, and then kept in orchards and little
" closes near home, with skim-milk and barley-meal,
" wanting nothing from the mother. Very much the con-
" trary is the case with the mare and foal: the dam is
" taken out of work, and devoted entirely to its young for
" several months; while the cow is rendering one of the
" most wholesome and nutritious articles of life in the
" highest perfection, leaving her calf to grow up by a
" little artificial means. At two years old, both the steer
" and colt begin to work; neither are capable of doing a
" full day's labour; but which is most likely to be reduced
" in value by over-heating or exertion, I beg to refer to the
" diseases incident to horses already mentioned. I have
" heard of a great profit being made by purchasing colts, and
" keeping them two years, and then selling them at an
" advanced price: this plan may answer where colts are
" extra animals on your establishment, of efficient strength;
" but I know of no instance, of the business of a farm
" being carried to any extent by young stock only: most
" farmers have a colt or two, which they humour and
" play with for a year or two, and are, generally speak-
" ing, well satisfied to sell out at ten pounds advance on

" * *Receipt for Weaning Calves*—Let the calf suck the cow for a week or
ten days in small quantities. Skim-milk boiled; and given rather warm.
Teach it afterwards, by the finger, to drink the milk twice in the day : if
you cannot spare *much* skim-milk, a very little of it, mixed with oatmeal and
water, will do. If in a cheese country, give whey boiled with oatmeal.
Treat them in this way for three or four months, first entirely under cover,
and as the weather grows warmer, let them be allowed the run of an orchard
or small close. Calves dropt in February, March, or April, do well to wean."

HERTS.]   " his

" his original price. The bullock would equally turn to
" proportional profit as he advances in age, without so
" much risk and attention; whereas, the longer you keep
" your colt, the more you multiply risks. With regard
" to the proper breed of bullocks, the enormous price of
" fashion has prevented my using the Herefordshire and
" Devonshire, because I did not think their advantage
" over other breeds, nearly of the same bulk, warranted
" the increase of price. My practice has been, to work
" cows, heifers, and any animal of strength that will draw,
" and to wean calves of any breed, since stock has been
" at the high prices of the last few years; and if I had
" had occasion to have bought in bullocks for work, I
" should have given the decided preference to those of
" Glamorganshire, because I have seen them working
" on HIS MAJESTY's farms, with more ease and expe-
" dition than any others; and from not being fashionable,
" more weight was to be obtained for the money given
" than perhaps of any other breed.

" With regard to fattening beasts, I seldom tie them
" up till they are very forward in condition, and then I
" have found nothing equal to oil-cake, to finish them for
" market; and I regret that the dealers in that commo-
" dity have not rather put their great advance on the oil
" instead of the cake, as perhaps it could be better paid
" for in paint, &c. than in the productive food of ani-
" mals. My experience convinces me, that a bullock
" cannot be kept too warm while stall-feeding, provided
" he is not made faint with heat, to a degree to prevent
" his feeding, which, however, will not easily happen.

> " I remain, dear Sir,
>> " very faithfully yours,
>>> " GEORGE VILLIERS.

" *Hillfield Lodge, June 5,* 1802."

Mr.

Mr. PARKER, at Munden, has eight working oxen, which do well for ploughing ; he always uses six in a plough for his deep tillage, and these are equal to four horses : he thinks if the Hertfordshire ploughmen were disposed to walk out as they ought to do, that horses would be superior ; but with the men of the country, oxen are equal. In general, he works them till seven years old, but has till ten ; and though in their fatting they have not been equally fatted at all points at that age, yet they have still been profitable ; and he esteems no loss equal to the inconvenience of parting with a very good worker.

Mr. Doo, of Bygrave, has worked oxen for fifteen years : he began with bulls and stags, but they did not answer ; then with Hereford oxen, and some other breeds, but none have answered so well as the breed which he has lately worked. These oxen were bought at Northampton, and called Shropshires, with horns not very long, yet indicating plainly the long horned race : they step quicker, are much hardier, and in all respects do better than the Herefords with him. He has two teams of five each ; he works four, and always rests one. They are not good for carting, but of great use in ploughing. He works them in collars upside down : they plough from five in the morning to half past one ; later in the year, from six to two do their acre, and in the afternoon fetch home the horses' lucerne. They have at present (September) and all summer through, nothing but grass ; whereas the horse-teams have lucerne and oats. Mr. Doo has not the smallest doubt of their answering, on comparison with horses, for ploughing, though four are only equal to three horses. As to calculations of reducing the expense of horses by buying two-year old colts, and selling them to profit, he will not admit that the system *proves* more profitable than the common one ; it is a very hazardous

zardous practice : the teams kept must be more numerous, and accidents are more common with young horses than with older ones : it is a matter of luck in a practice depending too much on servants and labourers. Chances, accidents, and maladies, are all in favour of oxen ; and as to food, there is no comparison. They never have hay, except in spring sowing ; the rest of the winter they have engine-meat from the barns, with malt-dust.

SECT. V.—HOGS.

THIS animal Mr. BYDE considers as very profitable to breed, but not at all so to fatten, unless pork happens to sell well, and corn badly. He has a sow which, in the year 1800, brought at two litters 25 pigs, which he sold as stores for 57l.: 12 from the pea-stubbles at 3l. 12s. each ; the rest were younger ; and the same sow has now 12 more, to begin the account for 1801.

Lady SALISBURY has the wild breed, which comes to 48 stone. But a circumstance in which this excellent farmer has great merit, is the culture of lettuce, as a food, and a most superior one, for hogs: she has had 150 hogs feeding on lettuce in a burnet field, upon which plants also the swine were found to graze well. Lettuces are the best of all food for hogs ; Mr. STEPHENSON, the very intelligent bailiff of her Ladyship, assured me that they thrive wonderfully on this food.

Mr. PICKFORD, of Market-Street, breeds great numbers of hogs ; he has now (1801) near 200 : he weans them on pease and barley-meal. Winter-tares are of capital use in supporting them ; they follow the scythe to eat all that escapes it, and some also thrown to them, to make

up

up the deficiency. In winter and spring, Swedish turnips are excellent for them: but he has no opinion of potatoes: he thinks that turnips are better, and gained at an expense considerably less.

The Earl of CLARENDON's hogs are half bred; a Chinese boar and the large Berkshire sow: in a year and a half they will weigh 30 stone; they breed well, are very handy, and fat upon ground barley and whole pease, or ground, if dry enough: they are a breed that pay well for fatting, which is not the case with many others.

Mr. LEACH, bailiff to the Earl of CLARENDON, fattens the large Gloucester hogs; he has a lot of very fine ones, for which he sent into Gloucestershire. Some of them he thinks will rise to 70 stone.

Mr. SEDGWICK, of Rickmersworth, has tried many breeds of hogs, and thinks the Suffolk the best; that they are hardier, and fat quicker, and on less food; and breed well as to the number of their pigs.

Mr. PARKER, of Munden, has the Suffolk breed, and also the Berkshire; he has a high opinion of the former, but thinks they have been, like some other animals, bred too fine; for with a great disposition to be fat, they are apt to be rather deficient in litters; the Berkshire sows, on an average, bring more pigs: these breeds do very well *once* crossed. Mr. PARKER does not find that potatoes are at all profitable for fatting, though very useful for store-pigs.

————

SECT. VI.——DEER.

THE Earl of CLARENDON, justly considering that there is no more impropriety in converting one animal to profit than another, makes deer an object of husbandry.

As

As soon as the rutting season is over, or usually about the 10th of November, his Lordship selects from the herd the weak ones, some of which would probably die in the winter, and keeps them in a small yard that has a shed on one side, and a net over the whole against pigeons, &c. ; the spot very warm, and well sheltered. Their horns are immediately sawn off, the place is well littered, and they are fed at a very small expense on pea-straw, hay, &c. warmth making up for the want of better food. At times, during the winter, they have clover-hay cut into chaff, and if they do not eat it well, a little salt is added. They have always plenty of water, and are kept perfectly clean: much attention should be paid by the keeper to make himself familiar with them, that he may enter the place without disturbing them. The first week in March he gives them oil-cake, about half a cake each a day with chaff, which fattens them so quickly, that all are gone in May. Before killing, they have some green meat given, to take away any ill flavour from the cake, supposing such to be the effect of the food, for it is certain that the venison is exceedingly good. As to weight, a haunch usually weighs about 24 pounds; a brace is sold for 15 guineas: the skin, worth 2l. 2s. is the keeper's perquisite ; so that the value of a brace amounts to 17l. 17s. exclusive of some trifling articles. The purchaser sends for them.

His Lordship usually fattens nine brace : his whole winter stock rises to 350 head in a park of 250 acres, but much of it is thickly covered with timber ; 30 sheep and 10 cows also feed in it. The park consumption of hay amounts to 32 loads, being reduced to that quantity by the use of much browse ; all ash, elm, and Scotch fir, being brought for that purpose before faggotting, which not only saves hay, but improves the flavour of the venison.

I have from various information conceived, that breeding

ing deer for sale was a very unprofitable business ; but the
circumstance stated in this account, of selecting such as
would probably die, or be unprofitable to keep, places
the estimate of advantage in quite a new light : thus considered, the speculation seems a profitable one.   It is not
uncommon to hear of great winter losses of deer in parks,
for want of a system in which such can be applied to advantage : nothing of this sort can be well done, that is not
in a regular course ; but, by this practice, every deer
which from severity of season, or from accident, would
be lost, is converted to a great profit ; as in such cases
the expense of fatting is a trifle, the greater burthen
of bringing them to an age for sale not belonging
to the account of this system.   Some have fattened
well that have had their legs broken by accident.   On
the manure being mentioned, I made the common objection, that deer's dung is good for nothing ; but this
Lord CLARENDON conceives to be a great error : his
Lordship had an experiment made to ascertain it ; he manured for turnips, three lands ; one with stable dung, one
with deer's dung, and one without manure ; the two manured were nearly equal, if any difference, it was in favour
of the deer ; the other of course was much inferior. There
are loop-holes in the fence, through which they are shot

SECT. VII.—POULTRY.

It was found at the Grove, that the poultry being confined to yards suffered much by the roop, and other distempers ; to remedy this, they have been kept in a different system. In April, and for six months, they are kept in
coops on four wheels, about twelve feet long, and two feet
and

and a half wide, boarded on one side, and open on the
other, like a common coop; the roof is of boards; a door
on hinges lets up for locking, to prevent stealing; uncommon success follows this method : a boy attends regularly against hawks. Lord CLARENDON has many of
these coops : turkies, guinea-fowls, ducks, &c. &c. bred
in great profusion. The conveniences in the poultry-yard
are numerous and well contrived; distinct houses for
geese, turkies, ducks, and fowls, and their roosts all diagonally varying from the perpendicular, so as to prevent
their dunging on one another.

CHAP. XIV.

RURAL ECONOMY.

SECT. I.—LABOUR.

" GREAT part of the labour of farmers is per-
" formed by annual domestic servants, whose labour com-
" mences and ceases at no stated hours. Day labourers
" work from six to six in the summer, and from seven
" to five in the winter ; their usual wages is 8s. per week
" in the summer, and 6s. in the winter. Labour per-
" formed by the great or piece is, hedging or ditching, by
" the 18 feet or statute pole ; felling timber, by the load
" (50 cubic feet) ; cutting underwoods, by the cord of
" stackwood, and brush faggots by the hundred ; thresh-
" ing and winnowing, by the load or quarter ; and mow-
" ing or shearing, by the acre. Much of the harvest
" work of that part of the county next London is per-
" formed by labourers whose residence is in distant parts,
" and where the harvest is generally later than in Hert-
" fordshire. The price of hay and corn harvest work,
" by the piece or acre, differs much in different years ;
" in wet and uncertain harvest weather, or when the
" crops in general ripen nearly about the same time, or
" ripen together, the price of labour, by the day or piece,
" increases : labourers hired for the harvest month have
" generally food, lodging, and two guineas for that time.
" The wages of annual servants are nearly as follows : of
" a carter or ploughman, from six guineas to nine gui-
                                                    " neas;

" neas; of a thresher or tasker, from six guineas to seven
" guineas; their task is five bushels per day, and they
" are paid at the rate of 1s. for every five bushels extra,
" and 1s. per load for binding wheat straw for market.
" Boys receive from two to four guineas, and maid-
" servants about five guineas. Day labourers employed
" the whole year by one master have 7s. and small beer.
" and 9s. and ale, for one month in hay time. The price
" of piece-work is nearly as follows: of hedging only, about
" 2¾d.; of hedging, scouring, and edging the ditch, 6d.;
" of hedging and cutting a new ditch, two feet wide at
" top, one foot at bottom, and one foot six inches deep;
" 1s. per statute pole; of felling timber, 1s. per load;
" of faggoting, 2s. per hundred. Barley and oats are
" threshed by the quarter; wheat, pease, and beans, by
" the load of five bushels; barley, from 1s. 4d. to 1s. 6d.
" and oats, 1s.; and wheat from 1s. to 1s. 6d.; and 1s.
" for pease. Clover-seed, 5s. per bushel. For reaping
" wheat, they are paid from 5s. to 7s. per acre, and some-
" times more, if it is much laid; and 2s. per acre for
" binding, with ale and small-beer; and 1s. 8d. per acre,
" for mowing oats and barley * †."

1801.—At Sawbridgeworth, Gilston, &c. the farmers
pay from 9s. to 12s. a week the year round, and harvest
costs them for a labourer 5l.

At Ware, 9s. or 10s. a week are paid; but much work
is done by the great.

In harvest, Mr. BYDE gives two guineas and food to a
man for the harvest: he sometimes finishes in three weeks,
and even in two, or a little more; and allows 12 acres, or
perhaps 14 for a man. They begin work as soon as light,

---

* First Report.
† These prices appear to me to be extremely low; and should be now compared with the present county prices, and regulated by them.—H.

and at six o'clock have bread, cheese, and ale; at nine, a hot breakfast; between eleven and twelve, bread and cheese: they dine at half past one, and have beef or mutton, and plumb-pudding; at four in the afternoon they have cheese and ale again: all these in the field; and at night, when they leave work, they have a hot supper at the farm-house at eight; but if carting, at nine, ten, &c. On the Sunday, they have three meals.

Eighteen men and four boys harvest this year,

    90 acres wheat,
    84 ——— barley,
    26 ——— oats,
    40 ——— pease,
    ———
    240

a few acres excepted, which are cut by other men.

About Hatfield, 9s. to 11s. a week are given in winter, and until hay-time; some gentlemen give 12s. In hay-time they earn a guinea. For the harvest month, 5l. and some beer: when fed, then they receive only from 45s. to 50s. For mowing grass, they are paid from 3s. 6d. to 4s. 6d. per acre, and beer. Laid wheat costs 12s. and 14s. for the reaping only, as it is not bound for that price: some pay from 8s. to 10s. and the corn is bound as well as reaped. Mowing spring corn costs 3s. per acre, and beer.

About Watford, 14s. a week in winter is given: Mr. WANGFORD remembers the wages 35 years since at 6s.

At Berkhamsted, 10s. a week is paid in winter; but in 1795, only 7s. without beer either in winter or summer.

About Beachwood, it was 7s. a week, and is now 12s. in winter, and until harvest. For the harvest month, the labourers are paid from 42s. to 45s. and fed.

At Hitchin, 12s. are paid till harvest; a year since 9s.: within 12 years 7s. only were given.

At

At King's Walden, 10s. 6d. a week are paid.

At Gorhambury, &c. the farmers pay 10s. a week to hay-time; and 5l. for the month, with ale and beer in harvest.

At Cheshunt 12s. are paid, except at hay and harvest: Mr. RUSSEL has had months men at 3l. now 6l.; but they are not fed.

At Barkway 10s. a week is paid; 8s. were given. To reap and bind wheat has been advanced from 4s. 6d. to 8s.

The average of the county now varies from 10s. to 12s. a week.

The note which marks the rise from 6s. to 14s. in 35 years, is curious. I have memorandums of the year 1774 now before me, which shew that I paid 7s. a week at North Mims in October and November. This is not doubling in 30 years, but near it. Such comparisons are much wanting, to correct general assertions and erroneous systems.

CHAP. XV.

POLITICAL ECONOMY.

SECT. I.—ROADS.

THE roads of a county so near the Metropolis, can scarcely be bad: six great leading turnpikes passing through so small a district, would alone give this character, but there are many cross-roads nearly as good as turnpikes. The worst are found in the country between Pelham and Welwyn.

SECT. II.—MANUFACTURES.

THE county may be said, in general, to be destitute of manufactures; not entirely so; but it possesses none that demand particular attention. Plaiting straw is a resource for poor women and children, in one part of the county, and will be mentioned in the next section.

SECT. III.—THE POOR.

IN the present state of this kingdom, I must consider this object as the most important inquiry that can come under the attention of a County Surveyor. I was anxious for information that could be usefully applied; but in general, the county is in this respect a blank. Its vicinity to the Metropolis secures higher wages, and more constant employment, than in many other districts; and does

not

not entail the same necessity, for new resources, which is found in many other counties.

From Hockerill to Ware, Hadham, and Buntingford, I was concerned to find that the women and children had little or no employ at home : spinning does not increase, and the quantity done is very inconsiderable. The expression of the farmers was, " they do nothing but break hedges:" this is the fault of the higher classes.

About Stevenage, spinning has given place to plaiting straw, by which they earn three or four times as much

The same is to be found at Hatfield; but Redburn is the place where the manufacture is most prevalent; where women will earn 1l. 1s. a week, and where a pound of prepared straw is sold as high as 6d. After six weeks learning, a girl has earned 8s. a week; and some clever little girls even 15s. * The farmers complain of it, as doing mischief, for it makes the poor saucy, and no servants can be procured, or any field-work done, where this manufacture establishes itself. There may be some inconvenience of this sort, but good earnings are a most happy circumstance, which I wish to see universal.

At St. Albans I saw much plaiting : here are women that will earn 5s. a day.

Little or none is found at Watford; much at Berkhamsted; the beginning of this spring (1801), a good hand could earn from 14s. to 18s. a week, which was the price of thirty yards of twist ; but now it sells only at 4s. per score. Mrs. MUNS, at Market-Street, is a great purchaser : she buys the twist of the poor, and makes it up into various fabricks, chiefly bonnets. Luton, in Bedfordshire, is also a considerable mart for it. Black

---

* This appears to be very high indeed.—*MS. Note.*

The facts were too universally known in Hertfordshire, and the information too often repeated, to permit my doubting the truth.—*A. Y.*

lace

lace making has been carried on at Berkhamsted time immemorial; these fabricks, especially the straw, render the women averse to husbandry work, and are said to make them bad servants, from their ignorance of every thing else. It is, however, highly beneficial to the poor : a child can begin at four or five years old. Some men employ themselves in getting straw for their wives. Some women have earned 2l. 2s. a week; but that lasted only a short time. Straw-plaiting is a cleaner trade than black, but not white lace-making.

About Beachwood, &c. scarcely one labourer in a parish is the owner of his cottage. Their rent, with a very small potatoe garden, runs from 2l. to 3l.

At Dunstable, they begin to pick the straw at four years old; plait at five; and at six earn from 1s. 6d. to 2s. 6d. a week; at seven they use the instrument, and earn 1s. a day; some girls of ten years old earn 12s. a week; and one was named who at eight earned as much. Women can earn 1l. 1s. a week on an average. Some men and boys are employed in it, as much more wholesome employment than lace-making. The instrument for splitting the straw was invented about a year since, and has had a great effect; before, they were forced to pick small straws, and could neither make the works they effect now, nor execute any so well. It is highly beneficial to the poor, and has kept their rates down, with no other rise on account of the dear times, &c. than from 2s. 6d. to 4s.

There is so much plaiting at Hitchin, that they will not go to service; boys are here also employed in it.

Near Gorhambury a girl of twelve or thirteen was named, who earns a guinea a week.

It is without any doubt of very great use to the poor, and has had a considerable effect in keeping down rates, which would have been far more burthensome without it.

The straw from stony and heavy land, like that of Es-

sex,

sex, will not do for plaiting ; and if a crop produces much straw fit for plaiting, the produce of the corn is generally bad : weak straw under hedges and near trees, does best. They give 2d. 3d. and 4d, a pound for it, and sort it themselves.

Mr. PARKER, at Munden, built a wind-mill, such as in common would cost 400l. for grinding every thing that he wants for his family and farm. He breaks oats and grinds for his labourers, who find it highly beneficial to them.

At Abbot's Langley, Mr. KINGSMAN carried me to a labourer that seemed to come within the description of my inquiries, THOMAS ATKINS : he has with his cottage six acres, thus cropped this year : one and a half of wheat ; one and a half of barley ; one and a half of turnips ; and one and a half of fallow ; thus having half his land in fallow ; an uncommon exertion for so poor a fellow, to exceed the proportion of the common husbandry of the country, on account of his land having yielded three crops of oats the last three years of his predecessor. He has one pig ; but no cow or sheep, He pays 10s. an acre for his ploughing, but it is never done till the farmer has finished all his own work. His rent 10l. 10s. but he lets off a part of his house for two guineas. Wishes for a Welsh heifer or a few sheep, to make dung. He has my wishes too ; and the further one, that they were not barren.

I am glad to be able to register one poor man in the county who keeps a cow. CATLIN, at Fowlers, in Redburn ; who rents a cottage and two acres of grass at 4l. 10s. a year. He keeps a cow, a pig, and some poultry. Has nothing from the parish, though an invalid. He has brought up a large family, his wife having had eleven children.

The Earl of CLARENDON gives nooks and corners of his fields to his labourers for planting potatoes ; which they

they most thankfully cultivate, and find of singular use to them.

Mr. Smith, of Clothalbury, has for a few years past let his labourers plant their potatoes on his fallows *, which has been of great use to them ; and of late, some other farmers have done the same ; but the wheat is injured by it.

The Hon. George Villiers, who was so obliging as to shew me some philanthropic establishments of great merit, which he had made at my request, favoured me with the following abstract of his ideas on this subject.

" DEAR SIR,

" I am too much flattered by a reference to any ideas
" of mine, not to use my utmost endeavours to be as clear
" and explicit as the nature of the point in question will
" permit me to be : and I feel, give me leave to say, that
" you have a *double* claim upon me, for any assistance
" which it may be in my power to afford, both as a per-
" son whose acquaintance I have shewn an uniform dis-
" position to cultivate, and as one, who for a series of years
" has applied with unremitting pains the whole force of
" his talents to the service of the community †. I must say,
" however, that I am sensible to no small degree of diffi-
" culty, in attempting to suggest any thing new, or wor-
" thy of notice, to those who have been long in habits of
" deriving information from your *Annals*, or any other of
" the publications upon agricultural subjects which your
" name has sanctioned.

" At a time when farming was not so much a matter of
" fashionable pursuit and amusement as it is at present, the
" early habits of my life induced me to turn my mind to

---

* This is, and has long been, commonly permitted in my neighbour-hood.—*H.*

† I am happy in subscribing most heartily to the above opinion.—*H.*

HERTS.]   " the

" the consideration of it, and after the experience of some
" years, with what observations my attention to the sub-
" ject, education, and situation in life, enabled me to
" make, I began to look *practically* to the manner in which
" I could best, not only benefit myself, but the poorer sort
" of industrious labourers, who, from the nature of my un-
" dertaking, were brought daily before my view. I have
" more, therefore, to say on *this* branch of agricultural
" study, than on *experimental farming*.

" A dissertation on the poor laws would not, I fear,
" tempt many people to peruse it, as too much has already
" been *said*, and too little *done*, towards the clear under-
" standing, and correct execution, of that admirable code
" of laws as they now exist. I shall at present confine
" myself to the statement of the line of conduct I pursued,
" as a person largely paying to the poor's rates, and la-
" menting sincerely the great waste and misapplication of
" immense sums raised on that head.

" The state of my parish workhouse was such as must
" be truly unsatisfactory to a mind of the least considera-
" tion or humanity; it was let by contract from year to
" year, and was not sufficiently large even to *contain* the
" persons claiming shelter under its miserable roof !
" What arrangement then for *comfort* and *convenience*
" could be expected from such an habitation ? I found
" the aged and infirm ; the dying, and even the dead ;
" the young and able, the abandoned and the well-disposed ;
" modest want and indigent profligacy, all confounded in
" one wretched mass ! I attempted to form a committee,
" to superintend the management of the poor, instead of
" farming them by contract, and to regulate the expen-
" diture of the money raised for their relief. I was out-
" voted in the vestry. and the *contract system* was accord-
" ingly carried. This circumstance (from what I had
" already

" already too plainly seen) convinced me that my fellow-
" creatures called most loudly for some assistance; and
" since the contract system *was* to be pursued, I thought
" I could not meet the evils belonging to it so effectually
" as by engaging *myself* to be *the contractor.* I had not
" much difficulty in obtaining that appointment, as my
" terms were the most moderate. I expected in such an
" undertaking little gratitude, less praise, and no gain;
" but I was sure my mental gratification would pay me
" amply, if I succeeded in bettering, in *any degree,* the
" sad condition of so many miserable objects.

" My first point was to divide and separate the different
" objects for relief and assistance which presented them-
" selves before me. The lunatics to Bethlem; the sick
" and aged to comforts and medical assistance; the chil-
" dren to occupations by which they might hereafter ob-
" tain a livelihood; and, lastly, though not the least ob-
" ject of my consideration, to force as few as possible into
" the workhouse, and to use my utmost endeavours to
" encourage those already in, to have recourse to their
" own liberty and industry for their support. It is now
" nearly three years since I have undertaken the manage-
" ment of the poor of my parish, and though, from the
" high price of provision, I have been a very considerable
" loser, yet I have the satisfaction of seeing my plans for
" amending their condition, and *ultimately,* and indeed
" *very shortly,* reducing the poor's rates, promise success
" equal to my most sanguine wishes. The slothful drones
" dare not apply to me : the orphan and illegitimate chil-
" dren are daily working their own way by industry, to
" be by degrees no burden to their parish; and surely
" the best way of teaching them the value of their labour,
" is to give them the whole amount of their earnings, and
" require them, as far as they can, to maintain themselves

" out

" out of it.   I shall perhaps be told, that boys and girls of
" tender years cannot earn sufficient to enable them to
" contribute much to their own maintenance; to which
" I have only to reply, that however small their remune-
" ration may be, provided they are allowed to join those
" whom I will call *free people*, when compared with the
" slavery of a *common* contract workhouse, I find their
" emulation and spirit so much raised, that every month
" produces fresh and rapid improvement in the quality
" and quantity of their labour.   I have the instances of
" three large families, subsisting on parish relief, who
" had been born and bred up in the workhouse, and were
" totally ignorant of every kind of work, except making
" a little mop-yarn for the contractor (which was no
" great object to him, as he had probably made a safe
" bargain for clothing and victualling per head), and
" who now are most of them capable of supporting them-
" selves; and being once allowed to know the value of
" their earnings, they will not, we may presume, very
" readily return to the abject state of labour and confine-
" ment which a workhouse presents.

" Lest I should be carried to too great a length on this
" subject, I will only add, that the earnings I allude to
" are obtained in a woollen manufactory which I have
" established, and in agriculture.   Attention to religious
" duties, warm and clean clothing, and as much whole-
" some food as can be eaten without waste, is the basis
" of my treatment of those under my protection.

" I must now ask your attention to my general manage-
" ment of the industrious labourers on my farm, who,
" from the extraordinary high price of the necessaries of
" life, and the regulated price of labour, were incapable
" of supporting themselves and their families by their
" earnings: to relieve their want, without wounding
                                        " their

" their honest pride and spirit, became the anxious object
" of my consideration. Generally speaking, the Satur-
" day night's transaction of the labouring man is little in-
" deed to his own credit, or to the advantage of his fami-
" ly: the alehouse affording him short change for his
" weekly earnings, and the little shops short weight and
" measure in articles often of inferior quality for their
" price; I therefore regularly paid them, by their own con-
" sent, a portion of their weekly hire in *meat*, and other
" wholesome and comfortable necessaries of life, always
" bearing in mind, that bread and wheaten flour being
" evidently the most scarce and costly, ought consequently
" to be the most sparingly administered ; and I found by
" experience, that issuing mutton and beef to the labour-
" ing poor immediately from my own stock, as a farmer
" and grazier, that one half of the quantity of bread be-
" fore used was found sufficient for the support of their
" families, and that I was not a loser by retailing out a
" small proportion of meat at a price suited to the pur-
" chasers, as I still sent the prime pieces to Newgate-
" market, for the more luxurious consumption of the
" Metropolis.

" It may perhaps be said, that this plan can only be
" adopted by those farmers who have a quantity of stock,
" and whose farming establishment is upon a large scale ;
" but I beg to observe, that the smallest farmer might
" make nearly a similar arrangement, either by allowing
" his labourers to have the use of his kitchen, oven, &c.
" or by suffering them to partake, for the benefit of them-
" selves and families, of the bread and meat of the farm-
" house (at a reasonable deduction from their wages),
" which would give the poor man and his family advan-
" tages which very few cottages are enabled to afford—or,
" again, the farmer might take upon himself to bargain
" with

The Moveable Sheep-house of the Hon: Geo. Villiers.

Elevation of the end.

Elevation of the side of the Building.

Section of the Building crossways.

Section of the Building side-ways.

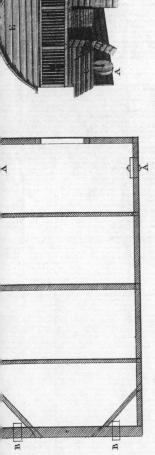

A. Wheels fixed to the axles 26 Inches diameter.

B. Wheels with Axletree to harness the horse to.

C. Weather boarded flaps hung with hinges, to turn up and button, against the sides when it is removed.

D. Folding doors to open when the sheep are let in or out.

E. Fixed weather boarding.

G. Over boarded Windows to open on hinges sidways in order to put fodder into the Racks.

H. Racks to hold the fodder.

I. Canvas Roof.　　K. Open railing for Air.

N⁰. The length of the building is from 20 feet to any length the width to be such as to enable the building to pass through the field gates, the weather boarding and flaps to be made as thin as possible, and covered with pitch.

The Hon⁰ Geo. Villiers Inv.

J. C. Varle sculp 35, Strand.

Elevation of the side of the Bui

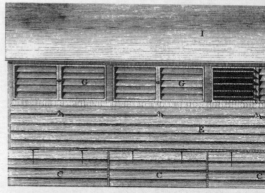

Section of the Building lengthw

Plan of the Building.

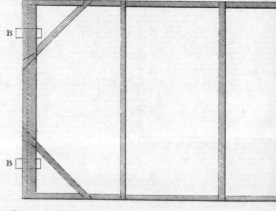

The Hon.ble Geo. Villiers Inv.

End of the Building.

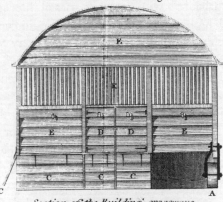

Section of the Building crossways.

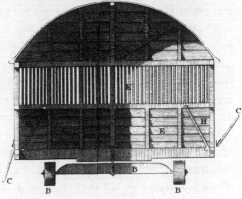

A . Wheels fixed to the sides 16 inches diameter.

B . Wheels with Axle-tree to harness the horse to.

C . Weather boarded Claps hung with hinges, to turn up and button against the sides when it is moved.

D . Folding doors to open when the sheep are let in or out.

E . Fixed weather boarding.

G . Cover boarded Windows opening on hinges sideways to put the fodder into the Racks.

H . Racks to put the fodder in.

I . Canvas Roof.   K . Open railing for air.

NB . The length of the building is 20 feet, the width to be such as to enable the building to pass through the field gates, the weather boarding, Claps, &c, as thin as they can be made. the outside is covered with pitch, the building may be encreas'd to any length.

S. L. Veele sculp 352 Strand.

" with a neighbouring butcher, or shopkeeper, to supply
" his labourers with the necessaries of life at fair weight
" and measure, *and at reduced prices*, in consideration of
" *ready money*, which might be stopt every week out of
" their, wages by their own consent.

" I also furnished myself with a cast-iron soup-boiler,
" from which my labourers, for a small sum, derived,
" twice a week, wholesome subsistence for their families.
" As there are at present so many receipts for soup known
" and approved of by the community, I deem it unneces-
" sary to enter further into the detail of the use of this
" article. But before I conclude these observations on the
" management of the poor, I cannot help lamenting to
" you, who I know to be zealous in their cause, that the
" office of overseer is blended with the occupations of
" persons carrying on trades for the maintenance of them-
" selves and their families, and that this important office
" is annually transferred from one to another. The *theory*
" sounds very plausible, that overseers are to find em-
" ployment for those who are capable of working; but
" look to the *practice*—what overseer or contractor, whose
" interest in the business, and whose powers of acting
" terminate at the expiration of twelve months, will in-
" stitute any trade, or use such exertions in forming and
" instructing children, as to enable them to gain a liveli-
" hood for themselves in future? The consequence is
" obvious; that rates are annually enormously increasing
" in most parishes, and with them, alas! the train of
" evils which they were intended to remedy. Living as
" we do, in the midst of the most opulent Manufacturing
" Nation in Europe, can we bear to see a race of people
" miserable from their poverty, and poor, only because
" they are uninstructed and unemployed, and not exert
" every means to endeavour to extricate them from their
                                        " present

" present state? a state of wretchedness to themselves, and
" of *worse* than inutility to the public.

" My anxious wish is, for a legislative act, to appoint
" an adequate salary for overseers of individual or united
" parishes, to recompense them for the time they *ought* to
" devote to that important avocation, and also to enable
" them to hold the office for a longer term than they
" now do.

" I remain, dear Sir,

" Very truly and faithfully yours,

" GEORGE VILLIERS.

" *Hillsield-Lodge, Feb.* 18, 1802."

CHAP. XVI.

MISCELLANEOUS.

I HAVE very little to register under this head; but one or two circumstances should not be omitted.

Price of Land.—The Watton Woodhall estate, sold by Mr. BENFIELD, produced 30 years purchase on the gross rent, and some part of it even more. Sir THOMAS RUMBOLD bought the estate, of about 5000 acres, for 85,000l. wood included : it lately sold for 150,000l. timber excluded.

At Hitchin, some land has been sold at 35 years purchase on the grass rent.

About King's Walden, &c. 28 years purchase has been given on commissioners' valuation.

Freehold now sells for 28 years purchase in general, in the south-west angle.

At Cheshunt, &c. freehold sells for 29, and copyhold for 24 : the fine, two years on a death, and a year and a half on alienation.

These are high prices, considering that the circumstance of farmers being the chief purchasers, which has raised land so much in some other counties, has not taken place here.

Experiments.—The experiment-ground of the Marchioness of SALISBURY was one of the most interesting spectacles which I saw in Hertfordshire. It is a field of 17 acres, thoroughly well fenced, surrounded with a margin of grass, and with two cross-walks, for the pleasing convenience of viewing the crops : they are well worth viewing, and do no slight honour to the talents of the cultivator. I here found

2 acres

2 acres ploughed after early pease,
2 —— lucerne,
7 —— cabbages,
2 —— carrots,
1 —— mangel wurzel,
1½ —— parsnips,
1½ —— coleseed;

——

17

besides two pieces, one of turnip-cabbages for seed, the other mangel wurzel, which ground had yielded a crop of lettuces for hogs.

In 1795 this experiment-ground was prepared.

1796. This year it produced red beets, mangel wurzel, parsnips, carrots, and cabbages.

1797. Half various sorts of cabbages, and half different roots.

1798. Where the cabbages had been last year, roots were grown, and after the roots of last year, cabbages.

1799. The same process was adopted, of reversing the same crops.

1800. Ditto, with the addition of pease.

1801. As described above.

Lucerne was added in 1800.

The cleanness of the crops, their flourishing luxuriance, and the general aspect of the whole, are truly pleasing. I could not, however, but regret that a register had not been kept of every crop, the expense, produce, and consumption per acre; this field would then not have yielded pleasure only, but an ample harvest of agricultural knowledge; and, with a few variations easy to have devised, would have produced a fund of important conclusions. The thought had great merit, and I cordially wish the field to be so productive of pleasure to its Mistress, as to give charms to the country, sufficient to rival the great foe to experiment—London.

The

The Expense of Cropping Seventeen Acres of Land, in the Year 1795, on the Experimental Farm in the possession of the Marquis of SALISBURY.

		£.	s.	d.	£.	s.	d.
7	Acres dunging, 15 load per acre,	26	5	0			
17	Do. ploughing, at 12s. do.	10	4	0			
17	Do. harrowing, at 1s. 6d. do.	1	5	6			
20	Bushels of potatoes, at 3s. 6d.	3	10	0			
24	Pounds of parsnip-seed, at 1s.	1	4	0			
24	Pounds of carrot-seed, at 1s. 3d. - - -	1	10	0			
6	Pounds of cabbage-seed, at 5s.	1	10	0			
					45	8	6
4	Acres of carrots hoeing and cleaning, - 30s.	6	0	0			
4	Ditto of parsnips, - 30s.	6	0	0			
6	Ditto of cabbage & beet, 20s.	6	0	0			
1	Ditto of potatoes, - 20s.	1	0	0			
2	Ditto of lucerne, - 20s.	2	0	0			
					21	0	0
17	acres						
					66	8	6
4	Horses five days ploughing up carrots, - -	3	0	0			
	Women for picking up and cutting ditto, -	11	3	6			
3	Days a team carting home ditto, - -	1	16	0			
4	Horses six days ploughing up parsnips, - -	3	12	0			
	Women for cleaning ditto, -	7	0	0			
4	Horses one day ploughing beet-root, -	0	12	0			
2	Men, six days each, packing carrots, - -	0	18	0			
6	Men forking carrots, 12 days each, - -	5	8	0			
3	Days a team carting home parsnips, - -	1	16	0			
6	Men forking parsnips, 12 days each, - -	5	8	0			
2	Men packing up ditto, six days each, -	0	18	0			
	Women cleaning and cutting beet-root, -	2	0	0			
					43	11	6
					110	0	0
	Rent of 17 acres at 30s. -	—	—	—	25	10	0
	Total expense, - -	—	—	—	135	10	0
	Profit. - -	—	—	—	462	10	0
					598	0	0

PRODUCE OF THE SAME.

		£.	s.	d.
1200 Bushels of parsnips, at 1s. - -		60	0	0
2560 Ditto of carrots, at 1s. 6d. - -		192	0	0
400 Ditto of potatoes, at 2s. - -		40	0	0
41,000 Cabbages, at 1½d. each, - -		256	0	0
200 Bushels of beet-root, at 1s. - -		10	0	0
10 Loads of lucerne, at 4l. - -		40	0	0
Total produce, - -	£.	598	0	0

Furze.

Furze.—His Grace the Duke of BRIDGEWATER has sown 60 acres of poor, flinty, gravelly, clay with this crop, for bavins, and it is supposed to answer as well, or better, than any common application of the same land*.

Markets.—At St. Albans, which is a market where they unload and set down their corn, every sack or load of wheat pays a pint to the Corporation.

It is the same at Hertford.

MOVEABLE SHEEP-HOUSE OF THE HONOURABLE GEORGE VILLIERS.

I viewed with pleasure, on the farm of this gentleman, the completest sheep-house I have any where seen, and therefore desired the favour of a drawing, which is here engraved, with the explanation.

* In Oxfordshire, near Banbury, they cut their furze every three years; and it will sometimes pay them as high as two guineas, and if I mistake not, sometimes even three, per annum, one year with another.—*H.*

THE END.